SPAIN

Spain

by Robert Goldston

The Macmillan Company
Collier-Macmillan Limited, London

FOR STEPHANIE VIENNA KARAKAS

The Macmillan Company,
866 Third Avenue, New York, New York 10022
Collier-Macmillan Canada, Ltd., Toronto, Ontario
Library of Congress catalog card number: 67-21248
Printed in the United States of America
10 9   8   7   6   5   4   3

PICTURE CREDITS: *Embassy of Spain, Information Department, 58, 64, 67, 70, 73,*
90, 99, (top), 99 (bottom); Ewing Galloway, title page, 5, 14, 24, 29, 34, 48;
Museum of Modern Art, 96–97; Radio Times Hulton Picture Library, 17 (top),
22, 52–53, 56, 57, 61, 77, 87, 102; Rapho Guillumette, vi (Brassai), 8–9 (Cash),
11 (Kit Robbins), 32 (Cash), 37 (Yan), 38 (Kit Robbins), 45 (Marc & Evelyne
Bernheim), 106 (Garrubba); Spanish National Tourist Office, 17 (bottom), 20, 35,
39, 55, 72, 105, 109, 114, 123; United Press International, 85, 118, 126; Wide
World Photos, 80–81, 82, 119, 127 (top), 127 (bottom). Picture research by
Patricia Crum and Sally Raymond.

Contents

chapter one

SPANISH EARTH

Spain. The very word rings like a trumpet blast through history. It conjures visions of proud *hidalgos*, heroic *conquistadores*, fierce Moors, fiery gypsies, the pomp of imperial courts, and the circumstance of battle. The names of its ancient provinces and cities—Old Castile, Aragón, Valencia, Andalusia, Galicia, Madrid. Seville, Toledo, Córdoba, Cádiz—have a golden sound. They speak of moat-girdled castles, of the gaiety of *flamenco* rhythms, of the solemnity of the bullfight, of galleons sailing to new worlds, of the treasures of the Indies. And yet these names bring other pictures to mind too: impoverished peasants, religious persecution, hungry workers, autocratic government, and years of ferocious civil war. To our minds there seem always to have been two Spains, the Spain of heroic legend and the Spain of grim reality. But neither of these Spains ever existed without the other, and today they are both in the process of dramatic change.

Cervantes (REAR) *looks out at Don Quixote and Sancho Panza.*

Napoleon, who could spot a paradox as easily as he could a weakness in his enemy's flank, once ruefully observed of Spain: "Africa begins at the Pyrenees." By which remark the great conqueror tried not only to reconcile some stubbornly irreconcilable facts, but also to excuse his inability to comprehend a proud nation. And Spain is, in fact, a land of paradox even today. It is at once the most Catholic and the most anticlerical of Christian nations. One of the richest areas of Europe in natural resources, it is also one of the poorest. It is either the most African of European nations or the most European of African lands. Inhabited by a fiercely independent and liberty-loving people, it has a highly autocratic and restrictive government. The paradoxes are endless, but the first, and perhaps the most important, is geographical. For the Iberian Peninsula, the shield-shaped land mass comprised of Spain and Portugal, seems itself to have been an uncertain afterthought in the construction of Europe.

Measuring approximately 540 miles from north to south and 620 miles from east to west, the peninsula appears firmly enough attached to Europe by a 250-mile-wide land bridge forming Spain's border with southern France. But this "bridge" in turn is almost completely blocked by the massive Pyrenees, a majestic mountain range averaging over ten thousand feet in elevation and traversed by very few, very narrow, and very easily defended passes. On the other hand, at its extreme southern tip, where British-held Gibraltar guards the gateway between the Mediterranean Sea and the Atlantic Ocean, Spain is barely ten miles from African Morocco, across a shallow strait that has rarely been a barrier to travel—or invasion. To the Spaniard proud of his ancient European heritage, Europe very often has seemed farther away than Africa.

A Land of Extremes

Between the snow-capped Pyrenees and the sun-drenched Straits of Gibraltar lies some of the most varied and dramatic

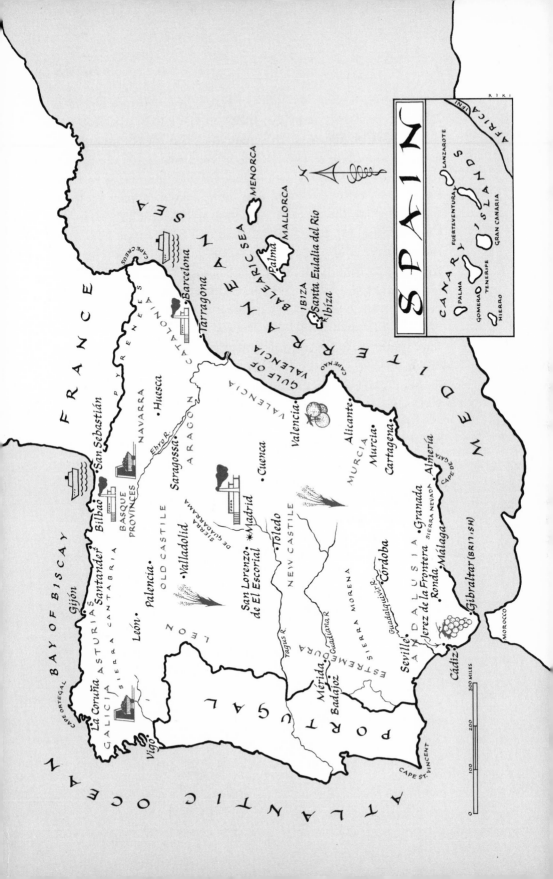

landscape in the world. Think of Spain as a great castle rising from the sea. More than two-thirds of the country is occupied by the Meseta, a large central plateau about two thousand feet above sea level. The Meseta is very flat, except for the abrupt intrusion of the Guadarrama Mountains that cut across it, separating the provinces of Old and New Castile. To the north of the Meseta on the Atlantic and Bay of Biscay coasts rises the Cantabrian range of mountains, which leads eastward into the Pyrenees. To the west, the hills and mountains of Estremadura separate the Meseta from Portugal. To the south rise the Sierra Morena and the Sierra Nevada (which boasts Spain's highest peak, Mount Mulhacén, 11,424 feet high), while to the east some of the most rugged hill and mountain country of Europe tumbles down to the Mediterranean coast. To the east and the south, this mountain-girdled Meseta is fringed by rich lowlands dotted with important harbors on both the Mediterranean and southern Atlantic coasts. But in the north the mountains fall so abruptly to the sea that only near the French border does Spain possess any important Atlantic harbors.

Spain's rivers, celebrated in song and legend, have been almost useless to the nation's economy until quite recent hydroelectric developments. The Tagus (566 miles long), the Guadiana (515 miles long), and the Duero (485 miles long) flow from the Meseta into Portugal. The Ebro (480 miles long) flows between the Meseta and the Pyrenees into the Mediterranean, while the Guadalquivir flows south from the Meseta into the Atlantic west of Gibraltar. Because these rivers are sunk into deep mountain canyons, they have been all but useless for irrigation purposes. None of them is navigable except the Guadalquivir, on which sea-going vessels can proceed sixty miles upstream to the city of Seville. While they represent a great potential source of hydroelectric power, their gorges and torrents make the construction of dams very costly. Only along the Ebro River has any sizable power complex come into existence.

The Spanish climate is as varied as the Spanish landscape. In the northwest—along the Atlantic coast and in the ancient

Basque provinces—it is a temperate marine climate with moderate year-round temperatures and plenty of rainfall. Along the eastern and southern Mediterranean coasts, from Catalonia to Gibraltar and including most of Andalusia, the winters are mild and moist but the summers are very hot and dry. The Meseta itself, cut off from the sea, has a Continental-type climate with cold winters (complete with snow) and warm summers. But the salient fact about Spain's climate is the lack of rain. More than one-half of the country has less than twenty inches of rainfall annually, and only 20 percent of the land receives as much as forty inches. It is apparent, then, how desperately the Spanish land needs widespread irrigation. On the Meseta the small farmers gaze hungrily at the unavailable waters of the Duero and the Guadiana, while in the southeast the peasants of Murcia watch their rivers and streams turn to dusty *arroyos* (brooks) during the hot summers.

Electric power plants on the Tagus River near Toledo.

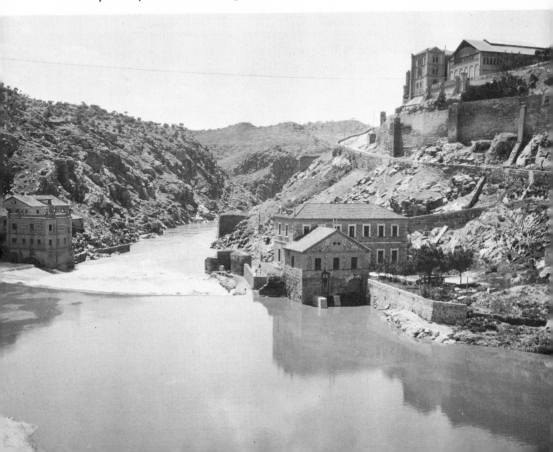

When the Spaniard looks around him, then, his horizons are sea and mountains. The immediate landscape is probably flat and dry, except for the narrow, lushly verdant southern coastal plain. Although his country contains only 194,884 square miles (about the size of Colorado), it has deserts reminiscent of the American Southwest, mountains like those of Oregon and Washington, and large areas as flat as Kansas. It is from these surroundings that the Spanish character has sprung, and from them that the Spanish people must wrest their living.

Natural Resources

Not that Spain is poor; only most Spaniards are poor. The average yearly income of a Spaniard is one-sixth that of an American—and one of the lowest incomes in western Europe. Yet no other western European country has such a variety of agricultural possibilities combined with so rich a subsoil. The second largest nation in western Europe, Spain has 42 percent of her total land surface under cultivation (more than twice as much, for example, as Great Britain). When this figure is compared to Spain's relatively small population (about 31,500,000), it gives a ratio of cultivated land per person that is far and away the highest in western Europe. More than that, the soil of Spain could be among the most productive in the world. Wherever there is enough water, the yield is extremely high. On the Atlantic coast, for example, where the rain is so heavy that it sometimes rots the wheat in the fields, the wheat yield is as high as in any hand-cultivated area in the world. And wherever else in Spain irrigation is employed, the natural yield of the land is rich. But unfortunately only a small percentage of Spain's land benefits from irrigation.

Water, a rare resource in Spain, is carefully rationed and controlled by the Tribunal de las Aguas. Water, or the lack of it, has given rise to more law suits and court cases than has the ownership of the land itself. In some villages of Aragón water is more expensive than wine. Only in the gardens of the old royal palaces (largely for the benefit of tourists) and on the private estates of the rich is water wasted in fountains. For a Spaniard, a fountain is the very image of a life of ease and luxury, and in most of Spain prosperity for the farmer means first of all a victory over aridity. It would seem then that Spaniards throughout their history ought to have concentrated their efforts on irrigating the land. But because of the difficulties of taming Spain's rivers, only large-scale cooperative efforts directed by the government could have succeeded. For a variety of reasons these have been undertaken only recently.

Nor have Spain's mineral riches brought prosperity to her people. She is the world's foremost producer of mercury (60 percent of the global total); the third largest producer of copper in the world; the sixth largest producer of iron. She is rich in lead, tungsten, zinc, manganese, and sulfur and has some of the largest salt flats on the face of the earth. It is true that Spain's coal resources are poor both in quantity and quality. And during the nineteenth century, when coal was the prime source of energy, this was a serious obstacle to the development of Spanish industry. But the example of Sweden, whose coal production is no better than Spain's but where a great modern industrial complex was created, demonstrates that planning and foresight might have achieved the same results in Spain. Now, however, after more than fifty years of indiscriminate exploitation for the benefit of a few rich families and, too often, for foreign investors, Spain's iron and copper reserves will soon be exhausted.

A divorce between man and the soil seems to be at the very root of Spanish poverty. For centuries the agricultural resources of the country have been laid waste. Deforestation and greedy cultivation—with no thought beyond immediate profits—have led to erosion. There is evidence that hundreds of years ago Spain was a heavily forested land. Today barely 5 percent of her area can be called true forest, and of this one-third is pine wood. Since 1953 about four million acres have been reforested by the government, but this well-intentioned effort is by no means sufficient. Thus, over huge regions, rain has carried away

A farm not far from Lorca in southeast Spain.

the topsoil. Along the Mediterranean shore, for example, about 40 percent of formerly cultivated land has been abandoned. While the history of man against nature in every country has been one of blindness, greed, and ruthless destruction of natural resources, it is in Spain that this conflict seems to have been most suicidal.

About two-thirds of Spain's cultivated land is planted in various grains. Wheat, which is by far the most extensively grown crop, is grown on the Meseta by laborious dry-farming techniques. Another 11 percent of Spain's arable land is devoted to olive trees (abundant in New Castile and in Andalusia), and 8 percent (mainly in the Castiles, Valencia, and Andalusia) is given over to the cultivation of grapes. Spanish wine is among the world's best, especially sherry, which got its name from the Andalusian town of Jerez where it is made. Other important crops include citrus fruits, sugar beets, and rice.

Besides having to work eroded and waterless soil, the Spanish farmer is handicapped by primitive methods of agriculture. Too often, whether the farmer be a small landowner in Castile or a day laborer on one of the great estates of Andalusia, he must break the hard, parched crust of the earth with a wooden plough not very different from that used by the Romans thousands of years ago. In practically no other country does the farmer have to work so hard to wrest a living from the soil.

Animal husbandry, which used to be of great consequence in the Spanish economy, is now of relatively little importance. Few farmers can afford to feed a cow (a pig, on the other hand, can be maintained with table scraps), and the raising of bulls—on the estates of Andalusia—is a business in which only the rich can indulge. In centuries past huge herds of sheep, under the control of a semiofficial association of sheep-raisers known as the Mesta, used to roam freely across the northern countryside. The herds laid waste all crops in their path, stamped the ground into dust, and stripped the bark from trees, thereby aiding greatly in the destruction of the soil. But the Mesta was dissolved by the decree of a liberal government in 1835, and, in

Breaking up the hay. The Spanish farmer is handicapped by primitive methods of agriculture.

any event, the reduction of Spanish grazing land made the sheep industry self-liquidating. Sheep are still raised in the foothills of the Pyrenees, but their contribution to the nation's economy is slight.

With a coastline of 1,300 miles (700 on the Mediterranean and 600 on the Atlantic), it might be thought that fishing and shipping would produce a substantial part of the Spanish income. Yet Spain's 110,000 fishermen, putting out in overaged and ill-equipped boats from the Atlantic ports of Bilbao, Santander, Cádiz, and Vigo and the Mediterranean harbors of Valencia, Málaga, Alicante, and Barcelona (and many a village in between), account for only 1.2 percent of Spain's gross national product. As for Spain's merchant marine, it is small (a little more than two million gross tons), and about 40 percent of it is more than twenty-five years old.

But although Spain may be poor, although her land may be parched, her mineral deposits nearly depleted, her landscape harsh and even hostile, she does have one great resource of which we have not yet spoken—the Spanish people.

chapter two

THE SPANIARD

In Spain October 12, which we celebrate as Columbus Day, is observed as the "Day of the Race." By "race" the Spaniard does *not* mean any pseudoscientific nonsense involving "pure" blood, nor does he intend to express any feelings of innate superiority over other peoples. On the contrary, he is celebrating the extension of Spanish culture to the New World and the mixture of the many peoples which have enriched that culture. For the Spaniard traces his roots to many different sources.

At the dawn of history Spain was inhabited by wild Iberian tribes that were most probably of Celtic origin and related to the peoples of prehistoric France. There are evidences of earlier races inhabiting the peninsula, going back to Stone Age times. But the Iberians (Celts) conquered or destroyed them (with the exception of one tribe, the Basques, whose claim to "Spanishness" is thus as well-founded and as useless as the claim of the North American Indians to "Americanism"). As the crossroads between Europe, the Mediterranean, and North Africa,

Spain was the natural focal point for a mixture of peoples—and it is from this mixture that today's Spaniard descends.

The Spanish Heritage

The first non-Iberians to arrive in Spain were the Phoenicians. These hardy sea merchants whose homeland was the coast of what is now Israel opened several trading stations on the Spanish coast near the sites of such present-day cities as Cádiz and Valencia. They traded Egyptian, Greek, and North African goods for Iberian fruits, grain, and olive oil. But the Phoenicians were not conquerors. They did not attempt to penetrate very far into the interior of Spain. They fought the Iberians when they had to, taught them something about the ancient civilization of the Near East, and, presumably, intermarried with them.

After the Phoenicians came their inheritors, the Carthaginians of North Africa. The Carthaginians were colonists and conquerors. They fought their way into the interior of Spain, wiping out the Iberian tribes that resisted, founding such cities as Barcelona, and settling down to mix with the native population. When Carthage went to war against Rome, her armies included regiments of Iberian infantry and Balearic stone slingers. The great Hannibal himself is said to have been born in Spain. But Carthage lost her struggle with Rome and lost her Spanish colonies in the process.

The conquering Roman legions came to stay. They succeeded in subduing almost the entire Iberian Peninsula and successfully colonized the interior as well as the coastal regions. They brought with them aqueducts, Roman law, arenas, roads, and the Latin language, which was to develop into modern Spanish. Roman rule lasted for six hundred years in Spain, and so thoroughly Romanized did the country become that, in the latter years of the Roman Empire, several of its emperors were Spanish-born.

The fall of Rome brought Vandals and then Visigoth "barbarians" to Spain. The conquering Visigoths, like others who

This Roman aqueduct dates from the time of Augustus.

had come to plunder, stayed to become civilized. They settled down and established petty kingdoms throughout the peninsula, adopting Christianity in the process and intermarrying freely with the native population. Blue-eyed, fair-haired Spaniards are not such a rarity (especially in the north) as is often supposed. They testify to the centuries-long rule of the Visigothic (Germanic) tribes.

One of the deepest impacts upon the Spanish ethnic heritage, and the one that sets off today's Spaniard from other Europeans, was made by the Moors. Crossing the Straits of Gibraltar in A.D. 711, the Moors, a tribe of North African warriors, carried the holy war of Mohammedanism into Spain. They conquered all but the northern sections of the peninsula. The reconquest of Spain by the Christian kingdoms of the north took seven hundred years. And all during that time, especially in the relatively secure southern sections of the country, the Moors were mixing with the local population and establishing Europe's greatest medieval civilization. The olive-skinned, dark-haired people of southern Spain, renowned for their grace and beauty, are the ethnic descendants of the long Moorish rule.

To this mixture must be added the contribution of those Spaniards who sought their fortune in the New World, married into various Indian tribes, and then returned with their families to the peninsula.

The Spanish Temper

Travelers often refer to German or French or American or Chinese "national characters"; but when they seek to describe the same quality in Spaniards they often use the phrase "Spanish temper." By this they do not mean the capacity for anger; instead they are comparing the brittle refinement wrought by thousands of years of unique historical development on the Spanish soul to the well-tempered blade of a sword—perhaps the famous steel blades of Toledo. This comparison is apt, for the Spaniard has been tempered by many centuries of struggle.

We have seen how hard the Spaniard must struggle to overcome the natural hostility of his land. In the course of this fight for survival against nature there came into being a hard, willful, and withdrawn kind of man. These qualities were hardened even further by a seven-hundred-year war against African invaders. This terribly long and costly struggle against the Moors, though marked by many famous battles, was essentially a *guerrilla* (little war) that was fought out on no fixed front but which might burst into flames at any time and any place. The Moors, fanatic in the cause of Mohammedanism and mounted on swift horses, might appear at any moment outside the walls of a city or a *pueblo*. Under the circumstances, every Spaniard—merchant, farmer, peasant, mechanic, lord, or knight—had to be something of a warrior. The Spaniard felt himself very much alone in the face of danger and was intimately acquainted with death.

This somber acceptance of death and danger has set the Spaniard apart from other Europeans. It is marked not only by

a certain fatalism in the Spaniard, but also in his taste for blood
sports, such as the *corrida de toros,* the bullfight, which is at
once a sport, an art, a pagan religious ceremony, and above
all an affirmation of man's ability to triumph over death. One
of Spain's great poets, Antonio Machado, has phrased this feeling:

> Today as yesterday, gypsy—you, my death.
> How good it is to be alone with you . . .

Self-reliance in the face of danger, awareness of death, and
a deeply individualistic outlook on life were not the only fruits
of the age-long fight against the Moors. That struggle also gave
the Spaniard a sense of mission. For many centuries the war
between Christianity and Mohammedanism was fought out on
Spanish soil, and the Spaniard came to regard himself as Christendom's first line of defense. This mission gave meaning and
purpose to his life. And when it ended in victory in 1492, he
discovered a new mission.

Only ten months after the last Moorish stronghold in Spain,
Granada, surrendered to King Ferdinand and Queen Isabella,
a Spanish lookout in the rigging of the *Santa Maria* cried "Land
ho!" as he caught a glimpse of a new world on the horizon. For
the next several centuries the Spanish mission was to conquer
and build that world. Perhaps only the centuries of warfare
against the Moors and the Spanish feeling of being the true
defenders of Catholicism could have enabled a mere handful of
men to subdue the great Indian empires of Mexico and South
America. In any case, when Hernán Cortés landed with three
hundred men on the Mexican coast he ordered all his ships to
be burned. To imagine that they might need those ships in
order to retreat would have been to question the reality of
their mission. Victory or death was the only acceptable alter-
native.

When the Spaniard can feel no sense of mission—of individual
importance—in what he is doing, he finds it difficult to accept
discipline. Without a Christianity to defend or a New World to

ABOVE: *Battle in 950* A.D. *between the Moors and the Spaniards.*
BELOW: *A Moorish fortress in the province of Granada.*

conquer he is likely to withdraw into himself. Yet in the modern
world, the Spanish mission, like that of many other peoples, is
simply the conquest of poverty, disease, and social inequality—
complicated goals that demand cooperation, patience, and compromise. To an independent and intolerant crusader these goals
and the virtues necessary to attain them might seem unworthy.
Thus, in spite of the fact that the Spaniard is technically
minded, an excellent mechanic, and as apt a pupil of the sci-
ences as any other nationality, he has seemed to be an exile in
a machine age based on social cooperation.

Any traveler in Spain will soon discover that Spanish indi-
vidualism and pride by no means prevent the Spaniard from
being the most sociable and hospitable of men. The need for
gaiety, for sharing his life with others, is only accentuated by
his heroic view of existence. A Spanish café is the gathering
place for friends, a talkative, lively, and informal club to which
all (even strangers and foreigners) are welcome. A Spanish
railway compartment is quickly transformed into a community
in which each traveler is expected to relate his life's story, to
involve himself, as courtesy demands, with his fellow passengers.
A Spanish home, however humble, is open to the world with
a hospitality found in few other countries.

The tourist in Spain who strays from the guided routes to
wander among the "picturesque" slums of a big city or the primitive streets of a dusty *pueblo* will soon discover that poverty,
lack of education, and a bitter struggle for existence have in no
way diminished the essential civility, courtesy, and pride of the
Spanish people. If the Spaniard is aware of being behind the
times technologically, he is also aware that he is among the
most civilized of men. He realizes that it takes only a few
months to train a good technician, but thousands of years of
history to produce a civilized human being.

The most apparent mark of Spanish civility is the formality
of personal relationships. Drawn from the Spaniard's need to
preserve his individuality, this formalism has come to make the
Spaniard view himself as an actor on the stage of history. The

drama is entitled "Life," and to play one's part with dignity and nobility is demanded by one's personal sense of honor. To give less than you have, to take more than you need, to say less than you mean, to boast of more than you can do—all these would be ignoble acts. If the Spaniard is something of a misfit in the modern world, he has reason to be proud of the fact.

Another aspect of the Spanish temper is somewhat less attractive: a certain spirit of intolerance, a quality of fanaticism regarding his deepest beliefs. To the outsider, the Spaniard seems to be continuously engaged in a crusade or continuously seeking one. This spirit of fierce partisanship also has definite historical roots.

The Eternal Holy War

According to Spanish legend, Christianity was brought to Roman Spain by Saint James the Apostle (in Spanish, *Santiago*) during the years immediately following the death of Christ. Though its followers were persecuted by the Romans, Christianity nevertheless quickly spread throughout the peninsula. Until A.D. 711 there was little to distinguish Spanish Catholicism from that of other European countries. But in that year the Moors brought the Holy War of Islam to Spain, and almost (but not quite) exterminated Spanish Christianity.

The fierceness and fanaticism that came to mark the Spanish Catholic Church is traceable, like so much else in Spanish history, to the seven-hundred-year war of reconquest against the Moors. Largely abandoned by the other Catholic states of medieval Europe during their long struggle against Mohammedanism, the people of Christian Spain came to look upon themselves as the only true defenders of the faith—and the only true interpreters of it. Spanish Catholicism was the only unifying principle to hold together the petty Christian kingdoms that battled the power of Islam. The reconquest of the Spanish homeland from the Moors was a religious as well as a nationalistic crusade. And Catholicism became inextricably linked with

nationalism and patriotism in Spanish eyes. It was fittingly symbolic that Rodrigo Borgia, Spanish archbishop of Valencia, should be crowned pope in 1492, the year of Spain's final triumph over Islam.

During the wars against the Moors, the only sure test of a man's loyalty to Spain was the quality of his belief in Catholicism. Thus religious faith became a test of patriotism. Atheism, freethinking, and nonreligious scientific inquiry could arouse the fanatic hostility not only of church authorities but of the masses too. Nor did this spirit come to an end with the national victory in 1492.

In the middle of the sixteenth century the Turks, by conquering the Near East and North Africa, raised once again the threat of an invasion of Spain from across the Straits of Gibraltar. It seemed the prudent and patriotic course to Spaniards to expel thousands and thousands of converted Moors from their Spanish homeland before they had a chance to become a Moslem fifth column. Only the great naval victory of Lepanto in 1571, at which Don Juan of Austria (half-brother of Spain's King Philip II) with a Spanish fleet sank three hundred Turkish warships and forever broke the offensive power of Islam in the West, brought an end to Spanish fears of a new Moslem invasion. But by that time the habits of fanaticism were too deeply ingrained to be eradicated.

The Inquisition had been imported into Spain in 1478, largely as a war-inspired security measure. Its function was to have been to test the loyalty (faith) of the thousands of Moors and Jews who had adopted Christianity under pain of death or expulsion. Frenzy and hysteria marked the Inquisitor's path. Thousands of converted Moors and Jews suffered torture, burning at the stake (the dreaded *auto-da-fé*), or, if they were lucky, expulsion. Under this religious reign of terror many of the ancient rights and liberties of the people had been under-

A procession in Seville during Holy Week.

Fire torture at the wheel during the Inquisition, which was brought into Spain in 1478.

mined and finally abolished. And when Moors and Jews no longer posed a threat, real or imaginary, the Inquisition turned its attention to Protestants and eventually to Catholic Spaniards who exhibited too much independence of thought or spirit.

The heritage of religious and intellectual intolerance in Spain is one of the factors that have held back Spanish progress in modern times. This heritage is also a deeply discordant element in Spanish national life, dividing liberal from traditionalist opinion, entering into the political life of the nation, and providing fuel for the fires of Spanish civil strife. Yet fanaticism is also, of course, the reverse side of that deep faith which armed the *conquistadores* who, with a handful of followers, overthrew the mighty Indian empires of the New World. Religion is and has been a source of both strength and weakness, and poses some of the still unresolved problems in Spanish life.

chapter three

...AND THE SEVERAL SPAINS

In the past people used to speak of "the Spains." Today they speak of Spain. Between these two references lie centuries of struggle and some important keys to the Spanish political scene today. More than 37 percent of all Spaniards speak two languages: Spanish and their own particular native tongue. In many of the more remote villages in certain areas, Spanish (which, because it is spoken in its purest form in the province of Castile, is always referred to as "Castilian") is barely understood at all. Indeed, to Basques and Catalans, Castile—the old conquering kingdom and since the sixteenth century the capital province of Spain—has often seemed like a foreign power bent on subjugating or "colonizing" the varied peoples of the Iberian Peninsula.

Are the Basques and Catalans to be considered non-Spaniards? By no means. Broadly speaking, they share the same history. Aside from the influence of their own languages, they also share the same culture. Nor are they as ethnically different from Castilians or Andalusians as they sometimes like to suppose. Above all, by economic necessity they are as much a part of Spain as are Castilians. Yet they cherish certain differences and have from time to time, under provocation and with indifferent success, fought for their independence. To understand Spain today it is necessary to know who these people are and why they consider themselves entities within the Spanish state.

The Tree of Guernica

In the north of Spain, from the western end of the Pyrenees along the coast of the Bay of Biscay to the city of Santander, lives a hardy little nation that calls itself (in its all but unpronounceable language) Euzkadi. To the rest of the world it is known as "the Basque region." While the most important Basque cities and the Basque provinces of Vizcaya and Guipúzcoa are in Spain,

Harbor and waterfront of San Sebastián, with nets drying in the sun.

nearly one-fifth of all Basques live across the border in south-western France. In Spain are an estimated 1,500,000. A large percentage of Spain's industry is located in the Basque cities of Bilboa, Vitoria, and San Sebastián, and the surrounding provinces are the source of much of the iron, lead, and copper to be found in the country. The Basque port city of Bilbao is second only to Barcelona in its capacity to handle shipping, and it is Spain's most important ship-building center. It is also vital to Spain's foreign commerce and, consequently, an important banking and financial center.

The Basques may be directly descended from prehistoric Cro-Magnon man. Most anthropologists agree that they are not, in any event, related to the other peoples of the Iberian Peninsula. Their language is utterly unlike any other in the world, though it has certain similarities to Finnish. The core of the Basque nation was never conquered by the Iberian tribes, or by the Romans, the Vandals, the Visigoths, or the Moors. When Charlemagne the Great sent his army into Spain, it was the Basques who fell upon its rear guard (commanded by Roland) at Roncesvalles in A.D. 778 and wiped it out.

The Basque Kingdom of Navarre was founded in 824 and included all the Basque provinces. But as the power of the Kingdom of Castile increased through the centuries, the Basques gradually lost their independence, until by 1512 they were wholly incorporated into Castilian Spain. Nevertheless, although subjects of the Spanish Crown, the Basques retained their ancient *fueros* (rights), which the Spanish king was obliged to recognize. The story of these *fueros* is a most important key to understanding recent Spanish history.

When the great Moorish invasions erupted into Spain, peasants, farmers, shepherds, city dwellers all found it necessary to place themselves under the protection of some local lord and his professional warriors. While they agreed to pay taxes (in money or produce) to him and, under certain well-defined conditions, to serve him, they also made sure that he would respect certain of their personal rights. Likewise, when the citizens of a

region or a city together with their local overlord placed themselves under the protection of one of Spain's kingdoms, such as
the Kingdom of Navarre, or Aragón, or Castile, they also made
sure that the collective rights of the city or region would remain
inviolate. The agreements, either between individuals and local
lords or between cities and regions and petty kingdoms, were
known as *fueros*—roughly translatable as "charters guaranteeing
certain personal and collective civil rights." Especially jealous
of their rights and ancient liberties were the Basques. Successive lords and kings who ruled over them had to go to the
Basque village of Guernica and, standing beneath the ancient
oak tree of Guernica (which may reflect even older pagan
rituals), swear to the assembled Basque people to respect their
rights, privileges, and liberties.

As the kings of Castile—through conquest, marriage, and inheritance—united the peninsula and became kings of Spain, and
as Spain became a great imperial power during the sixteenth
and seventeenth centuries, successive monarchs tried to modify
or revoke the ancient *fueros*. Over the centuries they were
largely successful. While Spanish *conquistadores* subdued the
Indian empires of America, Spanish monarchs subdued their
own people at home.

It has been a general rule of history that militarism and
expansion abroad lead to a loss of personal and civil liberties
at home, and such was the case in Spain. By the nineteenth
century only the Basques stubbornly retained their *fueros*. But
as a result of backing the wrong side in one of Spain's intermi-
nable nineteenth-century civil wars (the Carlist wars), the
Basque *fueros* were finally revoked in 1873. From that moment,
the Basques felt themselves foreigners in Spain, and Basque
nationalism became an active political force.

As the Industrial Revolution came to Spain during the middle
and latter half of the nineteenth century, it especially bene-
fited the Basque provinces. With their rich iron, copper, and
lead mines and the proximity of the coal mines of Asturias, a
large-scale industrial complex grew up along the banks of the

Nervión River, which runs to the Bay of Biscay through the port city of Bilbao. As Basque manufacturing grew in importance, Basques found that, because of the relative poverty of Spain's southern provinces, they could sell much less to other Spaniards than they could to foreign countries, especially England. Yet because of their prosperity, Basques had to pay a higher percentage of taxes to the central government than did other regions. Furthermore, the government at Madrid placed high import duties on agricultural products (which the Basques needed) and high export duties on manufactured products. So Basque nationalism found a solid economic basis that united both rich and poor behind a drive for independence from or at least autonomy within the Spanish state. As we shall see, this drive for independence both flourished and was finally crushed during the Spanish Civil War of 1936–39, but Basque nationalism remains a potent factor even today. Deeply Catholic by old tradition, relatively prosperous, industrious, and with a heritage of subdued but unforgotten democratic rights, the Basques sum up their feelings in the ancient battle cry: *"Jaungoikoa eta lagi zarra!"* (in Spanish, *"Dios y los fueros";* in English, "God and the old laws").

The Land of Gay Saber

From Valencia on the Mediterranean coast, north to the French border, and west as far as the city of Saragossa lies the region of Catalonia. It is said that the language of this region derives from the rough Latin spoken by the Roman conquering legions of Cato (Cato's Latin = Catalan). Certainly it contains elements of French and Italian as well as Spanish, but it is really distinct from any of these tongues. It is, however, very close to a now vanished language known as Langue D'Oc (literally "Language of Yes"), which was once spoken throughout southern France and coastal Italy as well as in Catalonia. In that language the phrase *Gay Saber* means "the poetry of Langue D'Oc," and in referring to their region as "the land of *Gay*

Saber" the Catalans mean to emphasize their loyalty to a more cosmopolitan and non-Spanish cultural heritage.

Until the thirteenth century Catalonia's economic and cultural ties were closer to France and Italy than with the rest of Spain. Catalonian commerce, language, and customs were based not on Spanish but on Mediterranean culture and trade. But when, in 1213, the Langue D'Oc people of France and Italy were all but wiped out in a savage crusade, Catalonia turned increasingly toward the rest of Spain, both economically and culturally. Its great capital and port city of Barcelona became the chief trading center between Spain and the eastern Mediterranean.

When, during the fifteenth century, the revival of Moslem power closed the Mediterranean to eastern commerce, Catalonia, like other Mediterranean regions, went into a decline. At the same time, as the kings of Castile became kings of Spain, what had been the semi-independent Dukedom of Barcelona was finally subjugated to the Spanish Crown. The opening of Atlantic trade routes to the Indies during the latter part of the fifteenth and early part of the sixteenth centuries completed the ruin of Barcelona's formerly prosperous trade.

The Catalan revival in the nineteenth century was due primarily to two causes: the opening of the Suez Canal, which once again established Barcelona as Spain's principal Mediterranean port and a prime trading center between Europe, Africa, and the Near East; and the harnessing of Catalonian rivers for electric power, which led to the establishment of a large industrial complex.

Like the Basques, Catalans now found that the poverty of the rest of Spain was an economic handicap. Catalan manufacturers had to seek foreign markets. Import and export duties imposed by Madrid worked against Catalan interests, and, although Catalans were but one-eighth of Spain's population, they found themselves paying one-quarter of the nation's taxes. Furthermore, progressive Catalan businessmen and manufacturers as well as the industrial unions that grew up among

Catalonia's workers found themselves hampered on every side by archaic and restrictive government policies. Modern Catalan nationalism springs, therefore, from many of the same grievances of which the Basques complain. An industrious, shrewdly commercial, very worldly and sophisticated people, the Catalans saw their independence movement and a good deal of their cultural heritage wiped out in the years immediately following the downfall of the Spanish Republic in 1939. But although their language was officially suppressed during the 1940s, it flourishes today, as does their drive for autonomy within the Spanish state.

In the longer view, of course, both the Basque and Catalan peoples are, and must be, an integral part of Spain. The independence movements in both areas are reflections of a failure by the central government to meet local needs and to create an over-all national economy within which the trade and industries of Bilbao and Barcelona can prosper.

The harbor at Barcelona.

chapter four

METROPOLITAN SPAIN

The Spanish environment is not, of course, one only of dry land,
deep-canyoned rivers, *arroyos,* and rugged mountains; it is also
an environment of thousands of small *pueblos* ("villages," but
literally, "peoples") and, increasingly, of large cities. Like all
Western countries, Spain is experiencing a population trend
overwhelmingly toward city life. Harsh living conditions in the
countryside have driven an estimated one million Spaniards
off the land and into the big cities during the past few years
alone. If the present rate of migration continues, by the year
2000 more than 80 percent of all Spaniards will live in a big city.

The *capitales* of Spain (so called by Spaniards because they
are the capitals of their provinces) are many and varied. Their
names have inspired poetry: Málaga, Valencia, Alicante, Seville,
Córdoba, Granada, Toledo, Madrid. But there is little poetry in
the problems of sudden growth which the cities of Spain share
with other cities from Moscow to San Francisco. A brief visit
to three of Spain's largest cities should make this apparent.

Madrid

Madrid, capital of Spain, has a population of more than 2,500,000 and is located on the Meseta, almost exactly in the center of the country. Like almost all Spanish cities it is divided into a new and an old town. Madrid reflects, in its layout and architecture, not only the fact that its chief product is government, but also the aggressive centralizing policies of Spanish regimes from the imperial court of Philip II to the present government of General Francisco Franco. It is the central point in the web of Spanish roads and railways. Traditionally all highways start in Madrid, and their mileage is figured from the Puerta del Sol, the capital's old central plaza.

Built by the Moors in the tenth century as the fortress village of Majrit, the city was captured for Christendom in 1083 by King Alfonso VI of Castile. But it remained little more than a frontier garrison town until Philip II made it both his personal residence and the capital of the Spanish Empire in the sixteenth century. With the arrival of the Bourbon kings in the eighteenth century Madrid was expanded and given a more cosmopolitan atmosphere.

The ancient Moorish and medieval section of Madrid, which nestles around the small hill on which used to stand the Moorish *Alcázar* (fortress, now the site of the royal palace), is a delightful place of narrow, winding streets, small plazas, and the remnants of Gothic architecture. The newer section of the city, dating from imperial days, is an area of wide boulevards, monumental buildings, and that dreary if useful checkerboard pattern of streets that has blighted almost all the cities of the world since the eighteenth century. There are several large parks in the city, such as the Casa de Campos (along the banks of the Manzanares River, which borders Madrid to the west and south), El Retiro Park, and the Parque del Oeste.

In Madrid you will find the ancient cathedral of San Isidoro and a new experimental atomic reactor station. You will find

The Gate of the Knife-Makers in Madrid.

such great national museums as the Prado, famous for its collection of paintings by Goya, El Greco, and Velásquez, and "American" bars by the dozen. You will find open-air markets to which farmers from the surrounding countryside bring their vegetables by donkey cart, and a subway system (the *Metropolitano*) suitably overcrowded during rush hours. Overlooking the Casa de Campos is one of the world's oldest universities (some colleges in it date back to the twelfth century), housed in very modern and efficient buildings in its own University City. Just a few miles out of town is the great American air base at Torrejon, where, to the delight of some Spaniards but the disgust of most, intercontinental nuclear bombers of the United States Strategic Air Command maintain their twenty-four-hour-a-day alert.

If you rise early enough in the morning in Madrid you may see a shepherd driving a flock of sheep to market down one of the wide avenues on the outskirts of the city and, a bit later, be caught in a traffic jam of cars, trucks, and buses on that same avenue. Perhaps symbolic of the paradoxes of this great city is the imposing palace, decorated with heroic statues, which houses the Cortés, Spain's legislative body. If you would hear realistic and interesting political discussion, avoid this building, which houses an all but powerless assemblage, and go to one of the hundreds of outdoor cafés that grace the city.

Madrid's population has more than doubled in the last thirty years. Migrants from agricultural districts continue to pour into the city at the rate of two thousand per month. In 1952 housing was in such short supply that an estimated eleven thousand people had to live in caves on the city's outskirts. Government housing programs have eased the situation somewhat since those days, but high rents and overcrowding remain the rule. Private investors have built acres of modern high-rise apartment houses on the city's edge, but these are intended for upper-middle-class or wealthy families or Americans. And so complicated is the tax structure and renting law in Madrid that many of these buildings remain closed—all wrapped up in red tape, Madrid's chief product.

Barcelona

Barcelona, Spain's second largest city and the capital of
Catalonia, has, according to government statistics, a population
of more than 1,650,000. But the people of Barcelona argue that
these figures are fabricated by the government to make Madrid
appear larger. This is but one of the suspicions (and the least
provocative) that Catalans continue to entertain about Castilians.

An ancient Carthaginian trading port, the city was known as
Barcino to the Romans. Remains of Roman walls, a tower, an
aqueduct, and a temple still stand in the older quarter of the
city. Barcino was taken by the Visigoths in A.D. 415, conquered

One of Madrid's oldest institutions, the Sunday market or Rag Fair.

The flower market on the Ramblas *in Barcelona.*

by the Moors in 713 (who renamed it Bardjaluna), and was finally secured permanently for Christendom in 995. During the Middle Ages the city was sometimes the seat of the independent Counts of Barcelona, sometimes ruled by a commercial oligarchy known as the Council of One Hundred, and eventually became the capital of the kings of Aragón. The days of Barcelona's maritime greatness were marked by such innovations as the Consulado del Mar, the world's first maritime code of law, and the world's first maritime insurance company, founded in Barcelona in 1535. Because of their proud maritime heritage (backed by a good deal of interesting evidence), Catalans claim that Christopher Columbus was, in fact, Catalonian and born not far from Barcelona.

The present city of Barcelona reflects the resurgence of trade and commerce that the city experienced in the nineteenth century. The great Plaza Cataluña near the city's center is rimmed by imposing banks and commercial office buildings. One of the world's most pleasant avenues, the Ramblas, leads from the waterfront into the Plaza Cataluña. A tree-studded central mall on this boulevard is the scene of colorful flower and bird markets on certain days of the week and the site of the *paseo* (literally "the walk," actually an all but ritualistic stroll made by the entire family dressed in their best clothes) every evening. The Ramblas divides Barcelona (from waterfront to the Plaza Cataluña) into a Gothic Quarter and the so-called Chinese Quarter.

The *Barrio Gótico* is a beautiful and peaceful section of the ancient city, dominated by the Cathedral of Santa Eulalia, which was begun in the thirteenth century. Its winding, narrow streets are cluttered with antique shops and tourists. Above it one will find the Parque de la Ciudadela, seventy-five acres of landscaped gardens with a museum and a zoo. The *Barrio Chino* (so named because it used to be the site of shipping companies that traded with the Indies) is a ramshackle, slum-infested center of bars, dance halls, and less innocent diversions.

Further inland, beyond the Plaza Cataluña, spreads the solid, somewhat Victorian architecture that houses Barcelona's large middle class. This section has wide streets, individual houses, occasional high-rise apartment buildings, modern shops, and pleasant gardens. Here and there are to be found buildings designed by the great Catalan architect Gaudí in the late nineteenth century—marvelously original designs in which buildings seem to emerge from raw stone. The delightfully surprising buildings, stone animals, and mazes of Guell Park are also Gaudí's work, and so is the solemn and monumental Cathedral of the Sacred Family.

In and around Barcelona is one of Spain's principal industrial complexes. Drawing power from the new Ebro River Project, large factories produce machine tools, chemicals, paper, and textiles. The port facilities are large, intricate, and busy. Beyond the industrial ring are to be found jerry-built slums into which workers' families are crowded under appalling conditions. Here, as in Madrid, government housing has by no means kept pace with necessity.

None of Spain's other cities compare with Madrid or Barce-

Cathedral of the Sacred Family, by Gaudí.

lona in size or industry or in cosmopolitan character. They are rather like provincial capitals, slower paced, more intimate in nature, comprehensible to the average citizen in a way that the great metropolis is not.

Valencia

Valencia, on Spain's Mediterranean coast, is almost the archetype of what most visitors think of as a typical Spanish city. Spain's third largest city, it has a population of about 500,000. Its smaller manufacturing complex has not yet ringed the central city with either slums or smoke-belching factories. Furthermore, it is located in one of Spain's richest and most fertile agricultural regions. The *huerta* (literally, "garden") around

ABOVE: *A watchman guarding the vineyards against marauding birds, rabbits, and men.* RIGHT: *A typical house in Valencia.*

Valencia extends for many miles of irrigated fields. There are huge groves of lemon and orange trees, tobacco plantations, and large vineyards. The city's industry depends mostly on the processing and shipping of these local products as well as the manufacture of silk, chemicals, clothing, glass, and those marvelously decorated tiles called *azulejos*.

Valencia is a city built on a city built on a city. First settled by the Phoenicians, it was rebuilt and fortified by the Carthaginians, and later destroyed and built again by the Romans. Conquered by Visigoths in 413 and by the Moors in 714, it was briefly retaken for Christendom in 1094 by El Cid, Spain's great medieval warrior, and was finally conquered by the Kingdom of Aragón in 1238. During the thirteenth, fourteenth, and fifteenth centuries the city rivaled Barcelona as a seaport. Valencia's trade declined at the same time and for the same

reasons as Barcelona's during the seventeenth and eighteenth
centuries. But unlike the great Catalan capital to the north,
Valencia did not have the power resources to develop a heavy
industry in the nineteenth century.

The main section of Valencia lies a few miles inland from
the sea, along the banks of the Turia River. There is an old
quarter of the city which, from the fourteenth to the middle of
the nineteenth century, was enclosed by walls. Within this
quarter are to be found a fourteenth-century cathedral (in
which the Holy Grail, the chalice from which Christ drank, and
the cup sought by King Arthur's knights, is presently on view),
university buildings dating back to the sixteenth century, and
a satisfying web of medieval streets and alleys and pleasantly
shaded little plazas.

Modern (largely nineteenth century) Valencia is a city of
broad avenues and heavy Victorian buildings that seem almost
incongruous when planted among palm trees and brightly
flowering Mediterranean bushes. The influence of the long-
vanished Moors can be seen in the white and colored tile domes
of many buildings. Not so overcrowded as either Madrid or
Barcelona, Valencia still has its own housing shortage. Many
of the stolid nineteenth-century homes that line the radial
avenues of the "new" quarter have been cut up into tiny apart-
ments sheltering entire families in one or two rooms.

The Valencia of the traveler's fancy is not entirely legendary.
There *are* guitars to be heard at sunset; there *are* gypsy cara-
vans to be seen occasionally at the open markets; there *is* still
an impressive solemnity to the colorful religious processions
at Easter time; there *is* yet a very definite sense of ease, almost
of indolence, about a life lived amid quiet streets, beneath
ever-cloudless skies, punctuated by the lively gossip of outdoor
cafés, the seasonal excitement of bullfights in the local arena,
and the sense of historical continuity in one of the longest inhabited cities in the Western world. Yet the daily life of the
Spaniard in Valencia, like that of his compatriots in the other
cities of Spain, is undergoing rapid and dramatic change.

chapter five

DAILY LIFE

The factor of change in the daily life of Spain makes generalization difficult. A small *pueblo* in Andalusia may exhibit a life essentially unchanged from that of the Middle Ages, while only a few miles away another *pueblo*, under the influence of tourism or of a newly established industry, may be undergoing the social birth pangs of a very up-to-date way of life. Government attempts to raise rural standards of living are also of great relevance; if a community has been incorporated in the expanding grid of Spain's rural electrification program, its way of life will naturally be much different from a *pueblo* in which power is still manual or animal. Regional differences are also important. The rhythm of life in a storm-swept Galician fishing village is far different from that of a sunny, palm-fringed coastal *pueblo* on the Mediterranean. In describing the life of a *pueblo*, we are taking a still photograph of a moving object. It is also a composite photograph.

The physical changes of countryside *pueblos* are matched in the large cities by the shifting kaleidoscope of classes. The life of a worker, of a small, middle-class shopkeeper, or of the very rich used to be fairly well defined and segregated. But the rigidity of Spain's social structure is now undergoing a severe shaking-up. Examples of city life based on class structure can, once again, be only selective and composite pieces of a richly woven tapestry.

Life in a Pueblo

Provided it has not been swamped by tourists and turned into a kind of Hispanic Disneyland by promoters and speculators (as have so many villages on Spain's Mediterranean *Costa del Sol* and *Costa Brava*), the Spanish *pueblo* looks much the same today as it did centuries ago. Certainly that noble and illustrious knight Don Quixote de la Mancha would have no trouble recognizing one, even though he rode out of the pages of a book almost four hundred years old.

If it is a northern *pueblo* in the Basque provinces or Galicia or in Castile on the Meseta, its buildings are made of yellowish brown stone cemented with mud. If is is a *pueblo* in Andalusia or on the southern Mediterranean coast, its buildings are constructed mostly of *adobe* (a sun-dried clay) and dazzlingly whitewashed. Unless a principal road runs through town, none of its streets will be paved. Until only yesterday its sewage system was all but nonexistent. In the south, a municipal water system was no more than a *seccia,* an open, stone-lined irrigation canal running through town. Drinking water is still hoisted from public and private wells or from cisterns that gather rain from the run-off on village roofs. The largest buildings in town are the church and the town hall (which also serves as police headquarters, jail, and barracks). The most popular buildings in town are those that house bars and cafés, of which there are many. In the smaller and more remote towns a local grocery, the government-run tobacco shop, or perhaps a bar serves as post office. One of the bars, or perhaps the rear of a restaurant, or sometimes the most convenient shed is used once a week as a dance hall and, if there is electricity, twice a week as a movie theater. You will see no television antennas sprouting from the rooftops, but you may be deafened by the number of radios going all at once and usually at top volume. Most probably there is no doctor in town, almost certainly no dentist, and there may or may not be a pharmacy.

Many people in town will keep chickens (which wander fairly freely, thereby developing enviable muscles that even hours of stewing cannot seem to tenderize), and the most fortunate will have a pig or two. Traffic will be dominated by donkey or horse-drawn carts with high wooden wheels, though the road may be disputed by an ancient automobile or two. In spite of these primitive conditions—or perhaps because of them—the *pueblo* will be remarkably clean on the outside (much cleaner than the average American small town, for example) and the interiors of private houses will be immaculate, a tribute to the strong backs of Spanish peasant women.

Most of the men in town work as farmers or peasants in the surrounding fields—farmers (especially in the north), if they are fortunate enough to own a small plot of land, peasants (in the south), if they go forth to work on one of the huge private estates of Andalusia, for instance. They rise at dawn, have a cup of bitter coffee, and trudge off to hours of heavy manual labor. At about 10:30 in the morning they will take a half-hour off to eat sandwiches (sausage or cheese or sometimes just olive oil) and drink wine from leather pouches called *botas.* Then they will work until noon, tramp back to the village, have a long lunch, and nap through the hottest part of the day. At about 3:30 in the afternoon they return to the fields and will work until six or seven in the evening. Before and after dinner the men will go to their favorite café, where they will nurse a cup of coffee, or a sherry or a glass of brandy, and play cards or just talk with friends.

The village children go to school at nine in the morning, after a cup of chocolate and perhaps a piece of bread smeared with olive oil. The school is generally a one-room affair in which all grades are taught by a single teacher. There are separate schools for boys and girls. After prayers and the singing of *"Cara al Sol"* ("Face to the Sun," the hymn of the Falange Party, Spain's only legal political party), the children commence their studies. The emphasis is on memorizing: reciting what you have read and learning the multiplication tables by rote, for example. A certain amount of time will be devoted to the study of the Bible and to Catholic doctrine. Aside from *what* is learned, *how* it is learned is much the same as it would have been in a rural American school of one hundred years ago. School lets out for lunch at 12:30 and starts again at 3:00 P.M. From then until school ends at 4:30 part of the time will be spent in learning useful crafts such as sewing and knitting for the girls and mechanics for the boys.

The village women have their housework (which takes endless time and tiresome toil without any of the electric and mechanical gadgets that have tamed the American home), the daily shopping, the laundry to do twice a week by hand, and most often some sort of work, such as sewing or embroidering, which can add to the family income. There are also the chickens and pigs to be fed and, often enough, work to do in the fields beside the men.

On Sundays and *fiestas* (holidays, of which there are *many* in Spain) the women and children (very rarely the men) will go to church in the morning. Later the entire family, dressed immaculately in their "Sunday best," will stroll slowly up and down the main street, or around and around the village square, meeting and chatting with friends, taking a glass of wine or the inevitable coffee at some local café. There may be a movie that night, perhaps a dance. The entire family (including babies sleeping peacefully through the noise in the arms of their grandparents) will go to the dance, where parents will keep a

A housewife draws water from a cistern in a house near Valencia.

strict eye on the activities of their young sons and daughters.

Fields and mountains, open blue skies, and uncrowded conditions in a country village do much to make rural life bearable. But unfortunately these natural advantages can do nothing to soften the harsh struggle that city life has long been for the average Spaniard.

Daily Life in the City

The life of a citizen in one of Spain's large cities is a continuing compromise between traditional custom and an intricate strategy for survival. Largely unprotected by his government-run unions, the Spanish laborer's income must go almost entirely for food and rent. He must work all day to earn the price of two pounds of meat; half a day to earn the price of one dozen eggs; one week to earn the price of a pair of shoes; an entire month to earn the cost of a cheap suit. He may own a radio, but the cost of such manufactured items as television sets, refrigerators, automobiles, and washing machines are far, far beyond his means. Although the cost of public transporation— buses, subways, and trolleys—is low (about five cents a ride) he will walk whenever he can. Although brandy and other domestically produced liquor costs no more than one dollar a bottle, he consumes much less alcohol than his American or European counterpart. Cigarettes cost about ten cents a pack, yet many Spanish workers save a few centimos by rolling their own.

Although his rent is usually very cheap, it is a strain on the family budget. And for it he gets none of the built-in fixtures such as a stove or a refrigerator which are generally included in an American apartment. The average Spanish family is smaller than an American family, but it is crowded into two or three small rooms and often includes three generations. Electricity, which costs more than three times what it does in the United States, is sternly rationed.

Under these conditions, the Spanish worker will, if he possibly can, either put in long hours of overtime or hold two jobs. If they have the skills, many laborers work the day shift in one factory and the night shift in another. A twelve- or fourteen-hour working day is not uncommon. Circumstances of family life make vast differences in living conditions too. Thus a bachelor, with only himself to support, is relatively better off than a married man. And if there are grown children in the family their working income helps mightily. Single women, the old, or the sick are most unfortunate because of gaps in the social security system and because women earn much lower wages than men, even for the same work.

Let's take an average family living in Madrid or Barcelona. The father is probably a semiskilled worker who puts in as much overtime as he can, perhaps working eleven hours a day. The daughter works either at some unskilled job (such as cleaning woman in an office building) or takes in sewing at home. The sons may well be apprentices and earning very low wages. The mother remains at home. This family is crowded into two or three poorly furnished rooms. Meat appears on the table once a week (in the Sunday *cocido,* or stew); oil and sugar are used sparingly. Each of the men in the family has one threadbare suit that is kept wearable by the ceaseless work and cunning of the mother.

Nevertheless, the formality of Spanish life dictates that every Sunday the young worker will appear on the street with an impeccably clean suit, bright white shirt, highly polished shoes, and an air of careless prosperity. For five cents he can buy a cup of coffee at his favorite outdoor café and has the right to nurse it all day long while he meets and talks with his friends. Once a week he will go to a soccer game (far and away Spain's most popular spectator sport, though basketball is now a close second) or to the movies. By saving up for weeks, a young man will occasionally be able to take his girl friend dancing; by saving for years he will one day be able to marry her.

In some ways better off than semiskilled workers, the Spanish middle class (a relatively small proportions of the population)

The sidewalk café is typical of the cities of Spain.

suffers from traditional adherence to outdated customs. Thus, a middle-class woman in Spain simply does not work; the very thought is slightly scandalous. Besides that, it is almost obligatory for a middle-class family to employ a servant, if only a twice-weekly cleaning woman. Middle-class sons are sent to college if at all possible, and the rituals of life—weddings, funerals, baptisms, saint's days (which are much more important than birthdays) are expensively and showily celebrated. The Spanish middle-class family is expected to maintain a front of prosperity and solid respectability no matter what the economic pressures. And since white-collar salaries and the incomes of small businessmen are only slightly higher than those of skilled factory workers, the strain is great.

Furthermore, the modernization of Spanish industry, the huge influx of tourists from wealthier lands, and the necessity to compete more efficiently have undermined the middle-class way of life. The American workday, which was adopted in 1960 by government decree, has made the long midday *siesta*, the leisurely lunch, the pleasant chat in a café during the afternoon only memories. And the sight of middle-class foreigners vacationing in Spain—able to afford travel, well dressed, often driving their own cars, amused by the "quaintness" of Spanish ways, and endlessly chattering of how cheap everything is in Spain—has given a bitter edge to middle-class ambitions.

But if the worker and the small businessman are relatively much poorer than their foreign counterparts, the rich in Spain are relatively better off. Because labor is so cheap they are able to afford hordes of servants, a luxury that has become impossible in other Western countries. Although a car may cost more than twice as much in Spain as in America, a chauffeur is paid a tenth of what he would earn in the United States. Spanish price controls, which because of poor administration, spotty coverage, and governmental indifference are not able to keep prices within reach of the middle class, *are* sufficient to ensure a remarkably high standard of living for the rich. Well educated, well traveled, cosmopolitan in taste and outlook, the rich Spaniard can afford not only the mechanical luxuries of the modern world, but also the personal service luxuries that the rich elsewhere have not enjoyed since the nineteenth century.

Spanish life, in the city as in the countryside, is undergoing rapid and dramatic change. Nowhere in the Western world are the paradoxes and trials of modernization more apparent than in Spain. Nowhere is the gap between rich and poor greater; Nowhere is the distinction between formal tradition and harsh necessity more painful. It is as if two Spains existed in the same country, struggling for the soul of the same people. And to understand this struggle and to hazard predictions about its outcome, it is necessary to understand the past from which it has emerged.

chapter six

THE IMPERIAL CYCLE

The history of Spain as a nation may be said to have begun on the fields outside the walled city of Granada. Here, in 1492, King Ferdinand of Aragón and León and Queen Isabella of Castile received the surrender of the last Moorish stronghold in Spain. Their marriage had already united their kingdoms, and they held the other petty principalities of Spain in sway. But although national history may be dated from this event, the history of the Spaniards, as we have seen, was already an old one. Many of those factors of Spanish history that have most puzzled outside observers are to be traced back to the unique seven-hundred-year war of reconquest against the Moors.

Of abiding importance as an inheritance from this epoch were the *fueros*, or charters of liberty, which we have already mentioned in connection with the Basques. An old proverb observes: from usage comes custom, from custom, the *fueros*. Reconquest was not simply a matter of winning battles. As

Catholic banners advanced across the Castilian plain against the Moors, colonies of soldier-farmers were established everywhere to hold the lands. These communes enjoyed personal and social liberties that were to remain unknown to the rest of Europe for many years. As late as the sixteenth century a mere local magistrate could set aside the king's orders if he so wished. Freedom of speech, of assembly, and the rule of common law prevailed—in all save religious matters. We have seen how the development of religious intolerance (due to the battle against Mohammedanism) undermined, in the sphere over which the Church had authority, many precious rights. But in the civil sphere it may be said that the *fueros* were the price that Spanish kings had to pay for the reconquest.

The Age of Conquest

The nation that came to birth outside the walls of Granada was hardy, full of soldiers of fortune seeking new fields to conquer, and expert in the military arts. It was also a nation in which, because the Crown had to respect their personal rights and communal liberties, the common people felt a deep commitment to the fortunes of the state. Spain was the first of the European powers to harness the energy and loyalties of her entire population to the nation's interests. Only in England and Switzerland, where liberties and the rule of common law were also emerging, could such a phenomenon be observed.

The amazing success of Spanish arms in Europe for the next century was due to a conjunction of several factors. First was the existence in Spain of a huge body of professional soldiers that had arisen during the reconquest. These men, known as *hidalgos* (from the Spanish *hijo de algo,* meaning "son of someone of consequence") knew only war as a profession. With the final conquest of the Moors, they flocked to the banners of the king of Castile, eager for any service on any battlefield. Since they were too poor to keep horses, they fought on foot. And it was just at this time (the end of the fifteenth century) that

The surrender of Granada in 1492.

the introduction of the arquebus, a light hand gun, made the old armored horsemen of European chivalry obsolete. The infantry was henceforth to be the Queen of Battles, and Spain possessed a huge and well-trained infantry. From Italy to Holland, from France to Austria, the Spanish infantry trampled down the armies of Europe and reigned supreme in the field.

Not that Spain purposely set out to conquer Europe. A series of dynastic marriages, inheritances, and bequests during the end of the fifteenth century more or less accidentally united the crown of Castile with the domains of the Hapsburg rulers

of Austria, parts of Italy, and Holland, which at that time
included Belgium. When the Hapsburg King Charles V was
elected Holy Roman Emperor in 1519, Spain was united with
the vast collection of petty German principalities also. But the
aggressively nationalistic tendencies of Charles' Castilian subjects may be measured by the fact that, although he was born
German Charles V and inherited the Spanish Crown among
others, the Emperor died Carlos I, a "Castilianized" monarch
who ruled his empire for the benefit of Spain. His son, Philip
II, was thoroughly Spanish.

Philip inherited not only vast domains throughout Europe, but also a huge empire in the New World. The fact that the Western Hemisphere was explored and conquered by Spain was not accidental. It was in Spain, during the centuries of Christian-Moorish strife, that Western learning came into contact with Oriental achievements that had been introduced by Arabian mathematicians, scholars, and doctors. Spanish scholars had made advances in mathematics, geography, and naval construction that placed them at least a century ahead of other European nations. Christopher Columbus therefore had to turn to the Spanish monarchy for support simply because none but Spanish vessels and Spanish mariners were equipped to venture out onto the "ocean sea." From the discovery of the New World in 1492 to the destruction of the Spanish Armada in 1588, Spain ruled triumphant at sea.

The hardy *hidalgos* who followed Cortés to Mexico and Pizarro to Peru, fighting against overwhelming odds with fanatical courage, conquered the vast Indian empires in an amazingly short space of time. They and their successors reduced the native populations of Central and South America to slavery and frantically exploited the gold and silver mines of an entire continent to enrich themselves and the Spanish Crown. It was this unparalleled wealth of the New World pouring into the coffers of Spain that financed the endless wars of conquest in Europe. These riches also produced a ruinous inflation and slowly but surely undermined the entire social structure of the nation. These effects, however, seemed unimportant to the subjects of Philip II, for they were embarked on that adventure dearest to Spanish hearts—a new holy war.

While it was true that considerations of power politics, economic greed, and international prestige were close to the root of Philip's wars in Holland, Italy, and France and his designs against England, this should not blind us to the essential sincerity with which he fought what he considered a crusade against Protestantism thoughout Europe. It was for good reason that the Pope bestowed on the Spanish monarchy in perpetuity the title "Most Catholic Majesty." It was this element of crusading fervor that helped inspire the common people of Spain to make heroic efforts toward victory.

Some understanding of Spain's age of conquest can be gleaned from a visit to San Lorenzo de El Escorial, where, at the foot of the Guadarrama Mountains, thirty miles northwest of Madrid, Philip built a royal palace that was also part of a complex of buildings including a monastery and a cathedral. Often personally overseeing the labor of his thousands of workers from a throne perched on a nearby hillside, Philip remarked that he was building a palace for God and a hut for himself. His small, sparsely furnished and severely practical apartment in that huge palace testifies to his sincerity. The long halls and exquisitely appointed reception rooms of the palace were purely functional. Here Philip received the ambassadors of foreign nations, tribute from subject peoples, and reports from his commanders. Here too he went over *all* state papers personally and made his plans to conquer England for the faith. And it was from El Escorial that countless orders demanding kindness and justice toward the subject Indians of the New World were issued (although uselessly) to Spanish colonists. It was here too, beneath the beautiful cathedral of El Escorial, that Philip and all his royal successors were to be laid to rest in marble

The royal palace apartment of King Philip II at El Escorial.

coffins. El Escorial has become through the centuries a shrine to Spain's glorious past—a shrine completed just as that past was to begin its slide toward chaos.

The Long Decline

The very wealth and extension of the Spanish Empire were the undoing of Spanish power. The gold and silver of the Indies created a severe inflation in Spain that undermined local industry and brought to ruin the small shopkeepers, artisans, and manufacturers of the cities. Furthermore, the lure of the American El Dorado caused thousands and thousands of Spain's most vigorous men to emigrate to the New World. Why should a farmer scratch out a bare living on parched earth when the riches of Peru or Mexico would be his for the taking? Why should the *hidalgo* seek employment when by following the

king's banners he could plunder rich cities in Europe? Nor were all the riches of America sufficient to keep the monarchy solvent. Philip was continuously in debt, continuously trying to raise new and more severe taxes to finance his worldwide ambitions (he considered them duties).

The truth of the matter was that Spain's power was built on a small population and a declining internal economy. The end was invitable. Philip himself lived to see his armies defeated in Holland (though they retained control of Belgium until the eighteenth century), driven from a France weary of the endless politics of holy war, and forced finally to accept the Protestant Reformation as a permanent fact. And when the vast armada Philip launched against Elizabethan England was sunk by Francis Drake and his "sea dogs" and scattered by winds in the Channel and the North Sea in 1588, Spain's rule of the sea came to an end. During the following centuries some-

LEFT: *Engagement between the British fleet and the Spanish Armada off the Isle of Wight, July 25, 1588.* BELOW: *King Philip II.*

"The Second of May," by the artist Goya.

thing of the shell of Spanish power remained, though continually declining. But under a series of ineffectual monarchs (Hapsburg until 1700, Bourbon thereafter) the sun of Spain's grandeur continued to set until, by the beginning of the nineteenth century, Spain had become a mere pawn in the brutal game of European power politics.

Spanish prestige reached perhaps its lowest ebb in 1808. In that year the Spanish king, Charles IV, who had been clumsily trying to steer a safe course through the Napoleonic wars, found himself a prisoner in France and was forced to abdicate in favor of Napoleon's brother Joseph, who was proclaimed king of Spain on the strength of three hundred thousand French bayonets. The ambitions of Napoleon, forced upon an all but prostrate Spain, had already cost Spain the vast Louisiana Territory, which the French sold to the United States in defiance of treaty obligations to Spain, and had forced the Spanish fleet to share in the naval disaster of Trafalgar. The occupation of their country by French troops and the casual replacement of their king by a Frenchman was too much for the people of Spain to swallow.

On the second of May, 1808, the people of Madrid rose in bloody rebellion against their French masters. Although the uprising was drowned in blood in the capital, it ignited a spark that soon enflamed all of Spain. The *Dos de Mayo,* celebrated ever since as a great national holiday, marked the beginning of the long and savage Peninsular wars during which, with the help of a British army under Sir Arthur Wellesley (later Duke of Wellington) and a nationwide *guerrilla* of unexampled ferocity, the French were eventually driven from Spain. It also marked the re-emergence into national life of those Spaniards who were devoted to the old *fueros* and influenced by the new political thought of the American and French revolutions.

With the royal family imprisoned in France, Spaniards had ruled themselves through local *juntas* (councils) during the Peninsular wars. In 1810 the *juntas* of Andalusia called together a national Cortés (parliament) at Cádiz. In 1812, after much debate, this parliament promulgated a constitution that, while it proclaimed Spain still a monarchy, gave to the Cortés the legislative powers enjoyed by parliaments elsewhere and severely restricted the power of the monarchy. But when, in 1814, the Bourbons, in the person of Ferdinand VII, returned to Madrid, it was soon clear that the constitution of Cádiz was to be completely disregarded. Monarchical tyranny settled once again like a pall over the country. This led to liberal elements in the Spanish Army leading a popular rebellion in 1820, but the rebellion was put down by Ferdinand with the help of one hundred thousand French troops.

The Spanish overseas colonies in the New World had chafed

for centuries under colonial policies that were at once terribly exploitative and ineffectual. Spanish colonies had been forbidden to trade with any other nation than Spain. But trade with the home country was much less lucrative than trade with the rest of Europe and the United States. Furthermore, this trade was beset with all sorts of regulations, taxes, and duties that strangled it. And as Spanish power declined at home, Madrid could no longer enforce its will overseas. To the ambitious Spanish colonists of the New World, the tie with Spain came to seem more and more a barrier to their development—and a tie that was tenuous at best. The economic motivations of the Spanish colonists of Central and South America were much the same as those that had impelled the English colonists of North America to rebellion. When Ferdinand VII tried to re-impose imperial authority over his subjects in the New World he was met by a wave of revolutions. By 1825 the last Spanish colony in continental America had won its independence.

The tyranny of Ferdinand VII was made barely tolerable to Spaniards, especially to the Basques and Catalans, in whom new tremors of independence were stirring, by the fact that upon his death he would be replaced by his brother, Don Carlos, who was liberal and had promised home rule to the Basques. But, by a somewhat less than legal stratagem, Ferdinand so arranged matters that upon his death his crown went to his daughter, Isabella. Thus, upon Ferdinand's death in 1833, Isabella was proclaimed queen of Spain under the regency (she was not yet of age) of her mother, Maria Christina. This was too much for Don Carlos and his followers. In 1834 they rose in the first of the civil wars known as the Carlist wars, which were to rend the fabric of Spain during the nineteenth century.

While the Basques may have been fighting for their ancient *fueros* in the Carlist wars, these struggles had a deeper and more widespread significance. They were the crisis points of the fever with which Spain emerged into a modern industrial world. The political, social, and economic problems of a Spain coming very late to the Industrial Revolution, to concepts of

SPANISH VILLAGERS RETREATING.

DON CARLOS.—AFFAIRS OF SPAIN.

[Th]e detention of Don Carlos as a prisoner in France was the sub-[ject] of a very interesting debate in the House of Commons on Tues[day] night; and which, in the words of the *Times*, has "tended to [thro]w a little light, a few sparks, into the dark chaotic mass of Spa-[nish] politics."

[Do]n Carlos, it appears, is at this moment detained in the Hôtel [Pame]tte, at Bourges, an ancient city in the department of Cher. [He], as stated by Mr. B. Cochrane in the debate of Tuesday night, [Don] Carlos is but meanly lodged. "He," Mr. Cochrane, "was at [Bour]ges in the course of last year, and had the opportunity of ob-[servi]ng the treatment of that prince. Whatever might have been his [cond]uct, he was a prince of the blood of Spain, and when he entered [Fran]ce one of the articles was that he should be always treated as an [esta]te. But what was the case? His expenses were limited to [£]0*l.* per annum—less than £700—irrespective of the rent of a [hous]e. He was lodged in most miserable rooms, having only [one] for himself; he might go out to a distance of four leagues, but [the] gendarmes and police always attended him. He had now been [near]ly four years shut up in that place, and had not been allowed to [hav]e a house in the town. His restrictions had become greater than [they] were at first, for when he (Mr. Cochrane) was there last year he [was o]bliged to have permission from the authorities of the town be-[fore] he was admitted to see him." On the other hand, Sir Robert [Peel] stated that he (Sir R. Peel) "was positively assured that Don [Carlo]s had enjoyed, and continued to enjoy, every privilege consistent [with] safety. So far from being imprisoned, he was permitted to go [four lea]gues from Bourges; he was permitted to visit at every house in [Bour]ges; he had even had the palace of the Archbishop offered him [for an] abode, and had he accepted that offer, he (Sir R. Peel) had rea-[son t]o believe that he would have been even still less subject to re-[strain]ts. These were the positive assurances which had been given

[Do]n Carlos is in his 56th year. He is the second son of King [Charl]es IV., and brother of Ferdinand VII., who died in 1833; he once

DON CARLOS.

had a fair prospect of succeeding to the throne of Spain. The king, his brother, had four wives, the last of whom, Marie-Christina, bore him two children, and these were daughters. By the provisions of the Salique law, adopted in 1713, by Philippe V., the royal succession was secured to Don Carlos; when the old king was persuaded by the in-trigues of the court, to abolish the Salique law, and to name the queen Regent, after his death, of the kingdom of Spain, during the minority of Isabella II. By this *coup d'état*, the prospects of Don Carlos were cut off; for he had every prospect of wearing the crown, when his niece, a child three years old, ascended the throne which he had so ardently coveted.

We have not space to follow the fortunes of Don Carlos in his at-tempts to establish his claims to the throne of Spain; more especially as the substance of his career will be found in the parliamentary de-bate already referred to.

Our other illustration represents an afflicting scene, now too fre-quent in Spain, viz., the flight of an entire village before a dominant leader; and a more sickening scene of the calamities of civil war can scarcely be depicted.

THE MAID OF DAMASCUS.

Aspettare e non venire, &c.—ITALIAN PROVERB.

To wait for those we love—
To wait and wait in vain—
To tread the appointed grove
And tread it o'er again—
Weeping—trembling—fearing—sighing—
Living on a hope self-dying—
Oh! there's no tardy, future bliss
That can atone for this—for this!
Methought I heard his step—no—no!
And yet 'twas something soft and sweet,
Which made mine ears mistake it so
For the first echoes of his feet!
They are the music that can bring
My heart-lute all its song again—
They have the magic pow'r to string
Its saddest fret to gayest strain!
But no! he comes not, and I'm left
Alone—forgot—perhaps bereft!   W.

A newspaper article on the Carlist wars.

social justice and mass participation in government, were far beyond the ability of traditionalist Spain to solve. Carlist wars, Army rebellions, seizures of power, abdications, even (in 1873) the very brief experiment of a republic, which was quickly crushed, were symptoms of political bankruptcy among the traditionalists. The solutions offered by Spanish liberals to these problems will be examined in Chapter Eight. But as the

Spain of monarchy, army, Church, and the rich, in spite of the establishment of a corrupt constitutionalism during the latter half of the nineteenth century, appeared impotent before the pressing problems of a new age, a growing divergence or polarity could be seen between the two Spains.

The final awakening from the ancient dream of imperial power came in 1898, when a bungling government in Madrid fell prey to the imperialist expansionism of the United States and lost Cuba and the Philippines, thus bringing the Spanish Empire to an end. On July 3, 1898, as the hopelessly outnumbered, outgunned, and underequipped Spanish fleet sallied forth to do heroic if useless battle with the powerful American squadron off Santiago de Cuba, Captain Victor M. Concas y Palau, commanding officer of the cruiser *Maria Teresa,* ordered his bugles to sound battle stations. "The sound of my bugles," he later wrote, "was the last echo of those which history tells us were sounded at the capture of Granada. It was the signal that the history of four centuries of grandeur was at an end and that Spain was becoming a nation of the fourth class."

Captain Concas y Palau was correct if somewhat belated in his appraisal. The imperial cycle was at an end. What was to replace it was the subject of increasingly bitter debate among Spaniards. The chaos of political life in nineteenth-century Spain can now be seen as the glow of heat lightning on the social horizon. A storm was coming in which the two Spains would hurl themselves upon each other with ultimate results that still cannot be clearly foretold.

chapter seven

THE LENS OF ART—
THE GOLDEN AGE

To understand a people, a nation in its history, it is at least as important to understand that nation's art as its geography or economics, and probably more important. Art is a lens through which the soul of a nation may be glimpsed and, insofar as it is truly great, the nature of all mankind. Over the centuries, no nation has made a greater contribution to the world's artistic heritage than Spain. And in no nation have artists been more directly inspired by the popular culture, the folk art, of their countrymen. Thus, if Spanish art serves to illuminate Spanish history on the highest level of expression, it has served also to express universal human aspirations and has given voice, more directly than in most countries, to the patient hopes and dreams of the Spanish people.

We cannot hope to examine here the life and work of all the many Spanish poets, painters, and writers who have en-

Miguel de Cervantes.

riched human culture, but by examining the contributions of the greatest, we may gain yet another perspective on this paradoxical land and its remarkable people.

Spanish Literature of the Golden Age

Spaniards have long been accustomed to regarding the sixteenth and seventeenth centuries as "the Golden Age" of their national history. It was during these centuries that Spain rose to the summit of imperial grandeur and power, but this age is remembered today as "golden" for the more lasting monuments of art it produced. Like the art of Elizabethan England, the art of Spain's imperial age is lusty, aggressive, energetic, and largely optimistic. It is the art of a people conscious of power, reveling in newly released national energies, seeking to sum up all of the human condition in their own experience.

Pride of place in Spanish art is justly given to Miguel de Cervantes Saavedra (1547–1616), who in his great classic novel *The Ingenious Gentleman Don Quixote de la Mancha* held up a mirror not only to the foibles of his own age and nation but to mankind throughout its history. Cervantes was an adventurer and a man of affairs; and it was his wide experience with men and events, from the greatest to the lowliest, that he poured into his work.

Cervantes was born of a poor family in Alcalá de Henares, a small town not far from Madrid. Although many of the facts of his early life are unrecorded, it is known that he studied at the College of the City of Madrid around 1569. During that same year he went to Italy, where in 1570 he secured an appointment as attendant to Cardinal Acquaviva. The next year he joined the fleet of Don Juan of Austria to fight the Turks. Though ill, he fought well at the great naval battle of Lepanto (October 7, 1571) and was twice wounded. His left arm remained useless for the rest of his life. But it may well have been the gallantry of Don Juan of Austria at Lepanto (in the face of universal indifference) that first inspired in Cervantes the idea of his forlorn and gallant knight Don Quixote.

After the battle, Cervantes returned to Italy, where he remained until 1575. In September of that year he took a ship back to Spain, only to be captured by Turkish pirates who sent him along with other captives to the dungeons of the Bey of Algiers. For the next five years Cervantes schemed and plotted various escapes from the dreadful slavery of the Algerian pirates, but all failed. It was not until 1580 that his family managed to scrape together enough money to ransom him. Thereupon he returned to Spain with justifiable hopes of a pension from the government he had served in peace and war. But like many another *hidalgo* of the imperial age, Cervantes found his petitions rejected by the monarchy, and poverty was to dog his footsteps all his life. In 1584 he married Catalina de Palacios, but the erstwhile adventurer found it difficult to settle into domestic life, and his marriage was not a happy one.

In 1585 Cervantes took a job as a requisitioner of supplies for Philip II's Grand Armada. But this thankless task brought him into conflict with recalcitrant peasants and sharp-nosed government inspectors, as well as with dispossessed priests whose property he had confiscated. His reward was a brief imprisonment (for "irregularities" in his bookkeeping) and excommunication from the Catholic Church (for having appropriated Church property for the monarchy). Finally cleared of the various charges against him, he applied in 1590 for a position in the Spanish colonies in South America. When this was refused, he retired to Madrid to live on the charity of the Count of Lemos and the Archbishop of Toledo, both of whom recognized his literary genius.

Over the years Cervantes had written in several forms—from poetry to essays. But his great masterpiece, *Don Quixote*, which was begun in 1605, was not completed until one year before his death in 1616. In this large and colorful tapestry of Spanish life, Cervantes poked fun at his own former pretensions and ambitions and drew a brilliant portrait of the common, day-to-day life of Spain. Cervantes' hero, the indigent *hidalgo* Alonso Quijana, is a great reader of romantic tales about knights and fair damsels and dragons and all the nearly obsolete paraphernalia of chivalry. Coming to believe in what he reads, Alonso adopts the name Don Quixote and mounted on his poor nag Rosinante sets out to right the wrongs of this world. He is joined by one Sancho Panza, a fat, shrewd, devoted, but extremely skeptical peasant who tries to dissuade him from his mad encounters, such as tilting at windmills under the illusion that they are dragons. After many adventures, Don Quixote's reason is restored to him; and, his head cleared, he promptly dies.

No more excellent parable of the pitfalls of idealism has ever been constructed. But while Cervantes made fun of the passing age of knighthood, he also mourned the gap between the real and the ideal in this world. *Don Quixote* was the world's first totally human novel. In it dreams are reality to he who dreams, characters have minds of their own, and throughout this magnificent tale the reader is made aware that to live is to let loose the capacity for all that is human. The art of Cervantes, like that of his contemporary William Shakespeare, was so over-powering that not only did all mankind find themselves reflected faultlessly in the mirror of his mind—his characterization of his fellow countrymen also provided them with a new environment within which their characters would ever after be molded.

A contemporary of Cervantes in Spain and Shakespeare in England was Lope de Vega (1562–1635). Born in Madrid, Lope de Vega attended the University of Alcalá. His stormy student career was capped by his being banished from Madrid for libel in 1588. An adventurer like Cervantes, Lope promptly joined Philip II's Grand Armada and sailed aboard the flagship *San Juan* to defeat and disaster in the English Channel and North Sea. Having survived this experience, he returned to Spain, married, and settled down at Valencia. But his wife soon died, and in 1596 Lope returned to Madrid as a secretary to the Count of Lemos (who was also befriending Cervantes). After 1603 Lope was employed by the Duke of Sessa. He had re-married, but when his second wife, Juana, died in 1613, Lope became a monk. His writing career was one of the most fabulous ever known. He claimed to have written 1,500 plays, and he certainly wrote at least 800 to 900, of which 470 have survived. About one hundred of these plays were each written in

Lope de Vega.

twenty-four hours. Furthermore, his poetry and other nondramatic works filled twenty-four volumes. Nor was this incredibly heavy output achieved at the cost of artistry. Early in his career Lope had won international renown for his wit and dramatic inspiration. In Spain the phrase *"es de Lope"* (it is by Lope) has come to mean "incomparably good."

Lope de Vega was the first Spanish playwright to conceive of the theater as a vehicle for pure entertainment, rather than as a stage for religious messages. He was the first also to create a drama, divided into three acts, in which the verse style was changed and adapted to accommodate the characters rather than to impose itself upon them. Although highly sophisticated himself, Lope made good use of the earthly quality of Spain's rich folk tradition, which was the essential source of his inspiration.

Nor were Lope's plays devoid of social significance. In fact, in the work of Lope de Vega specific criticism of social institutions makes its first appearance on the Spanish scene. In *The Dog in the Manger* (c. 1613), for example, he poked savage fun at the stilted attitudes of the Spanish aristocracy. In this play a noblewoman discovers to her horror that she has fallen hopelessly in love with a mere servant. Since this situation poses an impossible obstacle to a romantic attachment, it appears that the noblewoman's love must go unrequited. The problem is solved, however, by the servant's being passed off as the long-lost son of a nobleman; then, of course, his high-born admirer feels free to love him. Lope was not only mocking the pretensions of the nobility here; he was also pointing out that nature will triumph over social obstacles as well as pride.

In his later plays Lope often stood up for the peasantry against what he considered a corrupt aristocracy. That Lope saw the monarchy as the peasant's shield against rapacious nobles is indicated by the title of one of his last plays, *The Best Magistrate, the King*.

Inheriting Lope's position as Spain's foremost playwright, but disagreeing violently with his outlook, was Pedro Calderón de la Barca (1600–81), the last dramatist of the Golden Age. Born in Madrid, the son of a poor *hidalgo,* Calderón de la Barca was educated at a Jesuit school and studied canon law at the Universities of Alcalá and Salamanca. Leading a cloistered and uneventful life, he joined the priesthood in 1651. He was much influenced by the metaphoric style of Góngora, and his dreams dealt with such themes as freedom vs. imprisonment, passion vs. repression, and the fate of man's soul imprisoned on this earth. But unlike Lope, he saw man's only hope of salvation in dogmatic conformity to existing social codes of behavior. In his play *The Doctor of His Own Honor* the hero is forced to kill his own wife because she is suspected of infidelity. She is innocent, he knows, but he kills her anyway because she has been publicly suspected and hence publicly stained; and the code of honor demands that she die.

Calderón de la Barca wrote more than 111 dramas and many religious morality plays. He represented Spanish drama in European eyes and heavily influenced the birth of the romantic movement outside Spain. His plays are still extremely popular in South America.

Spanish Painting of the Golden Age

The Golden Age of Spanish writing was also the Golden Age of Spanish painting. And in the work of the Spanish masters of the sixteenth and seventeenth centuries many of the same themes that were dealt with by Spanish writers are expressed visually. The tension between heaven and earth, between the real and the ideal, between social criticism and social conformity all informed the compositions of Spanish painting.

Paradoxically, the first great Spanish painter was a Greek. Kyriakos Theotokopoulos (1541–1614), who was born on the Greek island of Crete, came to be known to Spaniards as "El Greco." As a young man El Greco had been trained in the Byzantine tradition of icon-painting. Moving to Italy in 1565, the young Greek established himself in Venice, where he came

"The Burial of the Count of Orgaz," by El Greco.

to know the work of the great Italian Renaissance painters Titian, Michelangelo, and Tintoretto. In 1576, hearing that the Spanish king, Philip II, was building a magnificent palace at El Escorial, El Greco went to Madrid in hopes of finding employment as an artist. But Philip II did not appreciate El Greco's talent, and the artist retired to the city of Toledo, where he lived the rest of his life.

El Greco's vivid colors and nervous, twisting, elongated forms were inspired by realism—but a realism of the spirit, not of the flesh. It is as if his counts and cardinals and even his cities were striving to achieve a union with God while still within their mortal coils. Employing mathematical concepts such as parabolas and ellipses in his later paintings, El Greco established the principles of what has become known as the "Mannerist" school of painting. His works, many of which are to be found in Madrid's Prado Museum, are perhaps the highest expression of the spiritual extremity of the Spanish soul.

Spain's greatest portrait painter and the recorder of the life of the imperial court was Diego Rodríguez de Silva y Velásquez (1599–1660). Born in Seville, Velásquez was influenced by the work of El Greco and also, from his two trips to Italy, by the work of Michelangelo and Peter Paul Rubens. A man of large ambitions, Velásquez managed to have himself appointed official court painter to Philip IV in 1623. His life thereafter was that of an imperial servant. In spite of the fact that he was eventually appointed Grand Marshal of the Palace (in Madrid), Velásquez found that he had to sit next to the king's barber at bullfights and other court functions—much to his mortification. But his dependence on royal patronage did nothing to blind Velásquez's sharp eye. His portraits of the Spanish royal family, aside from the brilliance of their style, are a coldly honest and terribly incisive look at the decay of a royal tradition. His princes and princesses gaze out at the world from cynical, indifferent, and hopeless eyes; his kings and grandees are monuments of sloth and mediocrity. The decay and eventual downfall of Spain's imperial pretensions are predicted in his work.

Toward the end of the seventeenth century, with the decline of Spanish power and the exhaustion of her people, Spanish art also went into a period of eclipse. The painting and writing of the eighteenth and most of the nineteenth centuries were remarkable for their heavy dependence on foreign themes and foreign influences. Not until the emergence of the so-called Generation of '98 was Spanish art to once again make new and important contributions both to the life of the nation and of the world. But before proceeding to examine the emergence of modern Spanish art, we must not overlook the isolated and tremendous contribution to the world of art found in the passionate work of one of Spain's greatest painters, Francisco José Goya y Lucientes.

Goya was born in 1746, less than one hundred years after the death of Velásquez, and died in 1828, more than one hundred years before the Spanish Civil War. His work is a unique bridge between the remembered glories of the Golden Age and the uncertain and terrible realities of the modern world. Goya was born of a desperately poor family of peasants and until he was thirteen worked in the fields of Aragón, outside the city of Saragossa. A rough and vivid personality, Goya loved the company of bullfighters, beautiful women, and adventurers. An early scandal forced him to flee for his life from Saragossa to Madrid. But he had not lived long in the capital before his boisterous escapades once again forced him into flight—this time with a group of bullfighters who were to tour Italy. No sooner had the group reached Rome than Goya once again found himself pursued by the police: back to Madrid.

Somehow, during these adventures, Goya found time to sketch his friends and surroundings. His sketches attracted favorable attention, and in 1776 he was commissioned to do

LEFT: *"Infanta Margarita," by Velásquez.* BELOW: *"The Duchess of Alba," by Goya.*

a series of cartoons of Spanish provincial life to serve as guides for a set of tapestries. The tapestries established his reputation as a fine artist, and by 1786 the brawling Goya found himself appointed director of the Spanish Royal Academy in Madrid. In 1789 he was made official court painter to the king, but his portraits of Charles IV were cruel, to say the least. Enjoying a stormy love affair with the Duchess of Alba during the 1790s, Goya drew two portraits of the lady in 1797—one nude, one (to fool her husband) clothed. But while painting high-born ladies and aristocrats Goya did not stop sketching the daily life he observed around him. His sketches satirizing royal and churchly abuses of the people's rights drew threats from the Inquisition. To these threats he remained literally deaf, since, during a visit to the Duchess of Alba in 1791, he had fallen ill and lost his hearing.

Goya witnessed the French invasion of Spain and the Peninsular wars against Napoleon. His drawings of that period, "The Disasters of War," eighty-seven etchings of unexampled realism and ferocity, are perhaps the greatest artistic indictment of war's cruelty that has ever been made. Later, after the war, he turned his talent to an even more terrifying series of studies called "The Disparities," which savagely illuminated many of man's universal stupidities. Disgusted by the reactionary policies of the restored Spanish monarchy, Goya went into voluntary exile in 1824 and died four years later in Bordeaux, France. His remains were finally returned to Madrid in 1919.

Goya not only bridges the emptiness of Spanish art between cycles; he also, in his development, sums up the past and predicts the future of the Spanish artist. In his early work Goya was content, like the great masters of the Golden Age, to observe and record both the good and the evil around him. But by the time of his death Goya was using his art as an active weapon, engaging it directly in the social struggle of his times. In the development of his work he seems to say that it is no longer enough for the Spanish artist to understand his world; he must now seek to change it.

chapter eight

THE SPANISH CIVIL WAR

Traditionalist Spain had made a mockery of constitutional monarchy during the nineteenth century. The game of fixing elections to the moribund Cortés, the meaningless shifting of "conservative" and "liberal" cabinets, all this was but the surface expression of a desperate attempt by a small group of Spaniards to stop the clock of history, to preserve their inherited privileges and powers. To the landowners and aristocrats who bought and sold elections and ran their estates as if they were feudal domains of the fifteenth century; to the bishops and hierarchy of the Catholic Church who enjoyed a complete monopoly of Spanish education, vast land holdings and rights that had been unknown to the rest of Europe since the Reformation; to the generals and admirals who regarded politics as their primary function; to the new class of large manufacturers who were determined to hold down wages and avoid taxes, to all these the Spanish constitutional monarchy provided an admirable screen behind which to exploit the Spanish people. But the screen first became transparent, then disappeared.

Alfonso XIII, who came to the throne in 1886 under the regency of his mother, was unable to provide an effective rallying point or even a front for the traditionalists. His government, undermined by riots, strikes, assassinations, savage police repressions, and finally, in 1921, by the terrible defeat suffered by Spanish forces in Morocco at the hands of Rif tribesmen, was saved from complete disaster only by the intervention, in 1923, of General Miguel Primo de Rivera, captain general of Catalonia. De Rivera, with the backing of the army, forced the king to appoint him dictator. But Primo de Rivera's dictatorship was in turn undermined by continuing resistance and also by the worldwide economic depression of the thirties. When the dictator went into exile in 1930, Alfonso XIII tried to rule once again through parliamentary means. But the municipal elections of April 1931 demonstrated that the king had no support whatsoever among the mass of the people. On April 12, 1931, Alfonso XIII abdicated and fled into exile in Italy. Two days later the Spanish Republic was proclaimed. With the traditionalists temporarily silenced, it was the turn of popular forces—the liberal Spain—to attempt to solve the problems of Spanish life.

Liberal Spain

Spanish liberals, counting among them small landowners, university intellectuals, certain junior army and navy officers, professional people, and part of the lower middle classes, had never abandoned the idea of a republic. Drawing part of their inspiration from the ancient *fueros*, but more from the development of democracy in France, England, and the United States, they hoped to establish a republican democracy and a liberal social and economic climate similar to that enjoyed by other Western nations. But Spanish traditions, Spanish poverty, and the uncompromising Spanish temper were all against them.

Furthermore, their ideas of democracy seemed insufficient to the vast masses of Spanish workers and peasants who had developed their own more radical ideas of how to reorganize Spanish life.

Two great movements had developed among the Spanish people at the turn of the century: anarchism among the downtrodden peasants, and socialism among the exploited city workers. Both of these movements were part of worldwide attempts to solve some of the problems arising from the Industrial Revolution.

Anarchism found its greatest following among the peasants, partly because of its easily understood program, partly because its extremely utopian aims appealed to the extremism of the Spanish temper. To the anarchists all government of any kind, since it was based on the use of force, was morally wrong. It was to be swept away and replaced by small local councils of workers and peasants who would cooperate voluntarily for the general good. There would be no more police, army, church,

King Alfonso XIII.

or state. To publicize their aims and to terrify their enemies, the anarchists believed in deeds of violence. Assassinations, blowing up of trains and buildings, and the general strike as political blackmail—these were the weapons of the dedicated core of anarchists. While there were only an estimated fifty thousand anarchist terrorists active in Spain, the movement itself enjoyed the support of millions and millions of peasants. But the anarchists had no more intention of supporting a republican government than they would have an autocratic one.

Socialists, who traced their origins to the teachings of Karl Marx, were opposed to anarchist ideas and also to middle-class republican ones. They believed that only if the people owned the means of production—the farms, factories, mines, and mills —and ran the government directly from this economic base, could true democracy exist in Spain. The success of the Russian Revolution gave a powerful impetus to socialist thought and socialist strength in Spain. It also led to a split in the socialist forces between those who sought to capture control of the state through democratic means (socialists) and those who held that only a revolution could bring their program to power (communists). Later the communists were to split between the orthodox, who followed the principles and directives of the parent party in Russia, and those who followed the philosophy of Leon Trotsky, the exiled Bolshevik Russian leader who clung to hopes of worldwide revolution.

To further complicate the Spanish political spectrum there was the renewed drive for autonomy on the part of Basques and Catalans and the ambivalence of peasant and worker attitudes toward the Catholic Church. Religion was a part of the Spanish soul, and especially among Spanish women, enjoyed deep devotion from all classes of the population. But the Catholic Church as an organization, because it had allied itself over the centuries with all that was most reactionary and repressive in Spanish life, had come to seem an absolute enemy to the hopes and aspirations of Spanish workers and peasants.

The new Spanish Republic, largely run by university professors, lawyers, poets, and Republican idealists, found it all but impossible to cope with the violently fragmented political life of the country. To deal with their enemies among the traditionalists they disestablished the Catholic Church, promulgating freedom of religious worship, withdrawal of government support of the Church, and the ending of Church authority over education. Various programs of land reform were aimed at the land-owning aristocracy. Statutes of regional autonomy were intended to please the Basques and Catalans. Dismissal of certain officers and a reorganization of military policy were attempts to suppress the political power of the Army. A new tax structure, along with the legalization of unions and strikes and the granting of other workers' rights, was intended to bring economic democracy.

But the Republic based its very existence on the support of the political parties of the left—socialists, anarchists, and communists—and it was far harder to deal with their revolutionary impatience. So aggravated had Spanish political tensions become that to Spaniards of the political left such measures as the granting of the vote to women, the establishment of a public school system, and so forth seemed too little and too late. Furthermore, the Republic, by its scrupulous devotion to democratic principles, left itself but poorly armed against its more violent enemies on both the left and the right.

The brief and stormy life of the Spanish Republic was one of continuous crisis. When the elections of 1931 returned a left-wing government, it had to cope with plots for armed uprising on the part of the Army-led traditionalists. When the elections of 1933 returned a conservative government, it had to cope with local rebellions in Asturias and throughout Andalusia on the part of socialist and anarchist workers and peasants. The suspicion and hatred with which the two Spains regarded each other led to constant riots, political assassinations, plots, and strikes. When, on February 16, 1936, new elections once again returned a left-wing government to Madrid, the forces of traditionalist Spain decided to act.

Loyalists charge rebel forces in the Guadarrama Mountains in August 1936.

The Rebellion of Traditionalist Spain

On July 18, 19, and 20, 1936, Army garrisons throughout Spain and Spanish Morocco rose in rebellion against the Republican government. The uprising, under the nominal leadership of General Francisco Franco, forty-four-year-old former commander of the Spanish Foreign Legion, had been long and well planned. The Army conspirators counted on the backing of Church leaders, industrialists, big landowners, royalists of various stripes, that percentage of the Spanish people to whom slogans based on past glory had some appeal, and the Falange.

The Falange (phalanx) was a semifascist political party founded in 1933 by José Antonio Primo de Rivera, son of the dictator of the twenties. Its program included repression of

workers' movements and popular political parties, the abolition of various personal liberties, absolute fealty to the Catholic Church and to the rigorous traditions of Spain's past, and an expansionist foreign policy. It had a small following, but its members were well versed in the arts of violence. Seeing in the Army rebellion an opportunity to further its own program, the Falange vigorously supported the Nationalist cause.

The rebellion was successful in Morocco, in various of the cities of Andalusia such as Seville, Granada, and Cádiz, in the province of Navarre, and along the Atlantic coast. But it failed in Madrid, much of central Spain, all of Catalonia, and the Basque provinces. Early successes against the surprised and unprepared Republican government brought the Nationalists—who had transported large elements (including Moroccan

General Franco (center right) with Colonel Ituarte Moscardo.

troops) of the tough Spanish Army of Africa to the peninsula
—to the gates of Madrid. But by late 1936 it was apparent that
General Franco's forces were not going to win a quick victory.
A long and bloody civil war stretched ahead.

Early in their campaign the Nationalists succeeded in enlist-
ing the support of Mussolini's Italy and Hitler's Germany.
Italian and German supplies, planes, technicians, and money
flowed to the Nationalists, and at least 50,000 Italian troops
fought under Nationalist banners. But while Mussolini was interested in securing "glory" for Italian arms and in the establishment of another Fascist power on the Mediterranean, Hitler
was concerned with simply keeping the civil war going as a
distraction from his own expansionist plans in Europe. Thus,
for the first few years, Germany never gave the Nationalists
the means of winning a speedy and decisive victory, but only
the means to continue the struggle.

As the Nationalists consolidated their territory, the kind of Spain they proposed to establish was revealed. High-ranking Republicans, trade union officials, and many of the common people who opposed them were court-martialed and shot. All political parties except the Falange were banned, newspapers were closed down, and attendance at Mass became all but compulsory. On August 15, 1936, in Seville, General Franco, displaying the old monarchist banner of Spain, cried to a large crowd, "Here it is! It is yours! They wanted to rob us of it! This is our flag, one to which we have all sworn, for which our fathers have died a hundred times covered with glory!" And it seemed indeed that mystical devotion to symbols and savage repression of opposition were all that Nationalist Spain had to offer.

The Revolutionary Republic

When rebellion broke out in that hot July of 1936, the trade unions and leftist political parties, recognizing the gravity of the threat to freedom, demanded that the Republican government arm the workers and peasants. After some hesitation the beleaguered government did so. Lacking organization and military experience and short of arms, the workers and peasants were yet able to put down the Army rebellion in Madrid, Barcelona, Valencia, the Basque provinces, and most of Catalonia and New Castile. In so doing they carried through what amounted to a revolution.

Wherever Republican forces were in control, big landowners lost their property, churches were burned, priests persecuted, and the entire apparatus of traditionalist rule dismantled. In Andalusia large areas were governed by anarchist militias, in Catalonia an autonomous Catalan government established itself, in the Basque provinces an autonomous republic was proclaimed. In many areas, Republican militiamen or enraged citizens fell on their age-old enemies among the rich with terrible ferocity.

The Republican military problem was to contain the Nationalist forces until the raw citizen-army could be properly trained and equipped. In seeking supplies the Republic very quickly found itself dependent on Soviet Russia. France and England, fearful of a possible war with Germany and Italy, maintained a policy of strict neutrality and nonintervention. Nor would the United States sell arms, gasoline, or other supplies to the legal government of Spain. The Western democracies were in the grip of the fever of appeasement. Only Russia and the international communist movement were willing to give substantial aid. The reasons for this were simply that Russia hoped to keep Italian and German forces involved in Spain and away from adventures in eastern Europe. For that purpose it was as much in Stalin's interest to keep the Spanish Civil War alive (while not providing the Republic with enough equipment and aid to win it decisively) as it was in Hitler's interest.

Russian aid, while never as extensive as German or Italian aid to Franco, was successful in preventing a quick Nationalist victory. Russian technicians, Russian planes, Russian tanks were all vital to the Republican war effort. Perhaps even more vital, at least at first, was the creation of the International brigades. These brigades of volunteers from many nations (including the United States, which was represented by the Lincoln Battalion and the Washington Battalion) fought heroically on many fields and often provided the margin of victory. But another and less happy consequence of the Republic's reliance on Soviet aid was the growth of the Spanish Communist party's power and influence.

The revolutionary Republic, which fought the civil war under a succession of governments, was idealistic and paradoxical. Republic ideals were expressed in the widespread program of public education (adults as well as children), in the liberalizing of Spain's restrictive social code, in the sincere attempt to give land to the peasants and control over their destinies to the workers, in the freedom accorded to political parties, the press, and individuals. More than that, Republican Spain felt itself in the forefront of an international battle against the growing menace of fascism. In November 1936, while the battle for Madrid raged, a Republican deputy of the Cortés expressed this feeling over Radio Madrid: "Here in Madrid is the universal frontier that separates liberty and slavery. . . . This is Madrid. It is fighting for Spain, for humanity, for justice, and with the mantle of its blood, it shelters all human beings! Madrid! Madrid!"

The Course of the War

The Spanish Civil War was one that engaged the emotions and attention of the entire world. It seemed to be a war of belief on both sides, rather than a mere struggle for material wealth. The personalities involved in the struggle became international heroes or villains. On the Republican side there were the peasants-turned-generals: Modesto; *"El Campesino"* (the peasant); Durruti, the anarchist leader; and Lister. There were the vivid personalities of *"La Pasiónaria,"* the former fishwife who

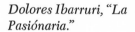

Dolores Ibarruri, "La Pasiónaria."

had become a brilliant and fanatic communist leader; Largo Caballero, the socialist prime minister whose son was shot by the Nationalists; Luis Companys, the dapper president of autonomous Catalonia; Prieto, the excitable socialist minister; and Juan Negrín, strongman of the Republic.

Nationalist Spain had its colorful generals such as Queipo de Llano, the garrulous "radio general" who made a practice of talking disjointedly over the radio to the world whenever the spirit moved him; Colonel Moscardo, the heroic defender of the *alcázar* at Toledo; General Yagüe, conqueror of Catalonia. But more and more the personality which came to dominate and completely represent the Nationalist cause was that of General Francisco Franco. Sober, industrious, extremely cautious, and politically highly astute, he managed to juggle Church, Falange, monarchists, and Army in such a way that all were subordinate to him.

With few exceptions, the war was a progression of Nationalist victories and advances. When Franco's forces were foiled in their attempt to take Madrid in late 1936, they turned to the conquest of the Basque provinces. And in spite of heroic resistance by the Basque people, they were crushed by Nationalist forces during the spring of 1937. One searing episode of the Basque tragedy was the bombardment of the defenseless old market town of Guernica by squadrons of bombers of the German Condor Legion on April 26, 1937. The town was wiped out and many of its citizens killed. This incident, which shocked and outraged people all over the world, moved the great Catalan painter Pablo Picasso to paint a picture entitled "Guernica," which many have judged to be his masterpiece.

During 1937 Republican forces won victories at Brunete, west of Madrid, and at Teruel in the north; but these successes were hollow, since the Republic had no means of following them up. In March Republican forces inflicted a stunning defeat on the Italian Army in Spain at Guadalajara, wrecking the entire Italian force, capturing thousands of prisoners, and making Mussolini the laughing stock of the world. But again this was basically, like all Republican triumphs, a defensive victory. In a strategic sense the initiative remained with the Nationalists.

One of the reasons for the failure of the Republican war effort was the constant bickering between the various left-wing parties that often broke out into riots and even (in Barcelona during May 1937) into a minor civil war within the civil war. Communists fought Trotskyites, anarchists fought all comers,

Spanish refugees escaping across the Pyrenees into France.

and socialists desperately tried to hold the government together. They succeeded, but suspicion, hatred, and outright
fighting in the Republican camp seriously weakened the war
effort.

The year 1938 saw heavy fighting on all fronts, with the
Nationalists cutting the Republic in half north of Valencia
and driving back Republican lines in western Catalonia. A
Republican counteroffensive on the line of the Ebro River
late in the year stabilized the front, but at fearful cost. It was
at this moment that foreign intervention in Spain proved decisive. By the fall of 1938 Hitler was convinced that the democracies would not fight. Therefore, he determined to give the
Nationalists enough arms and equipment to permit them to
win a decisive victory, just on the heels of the costly Republican
offensive at the Ebro. Republican supplies had been depleted,
and Russian aid was not immediately forthcoming. When the
new Nationalist offensive started in January 1939, it rolled
forward with surprising speed against scanty opposition. On
January 26, 1939, the Nationalists entered Barcelona. While
thousands and thousands of Republican refugees fled along the
roads north into France, General Yagüe, in the Plaza Cataluña,
proclaimed the end of the dream of Catalan autonomy.

On March 28 Franco's troops entered Madrid. By April 1,
1939, resistance was at an end throughout the peninsula. The
idealistic Republic had been crushed. Traditionalist Spain was
triumphant.

chapter nine

The Lens of Art— The Generation of '98

What was killed in 1939 was not only the political structure of the Spanish Republic. The dream of Spanish artists of the generation that had given rebirth to the glories of Spanish art was also crushed. Because so many of them came of age around 1898 and because 1898, the year of Spain's defeat by the United States, gave the urgency and impetus of shock to their work, the Spanish writers who came to prominence around the turn of the nineteenth century adopted the name "the Generation of '98." It was they who dreamed the dreams, argued the causes, defined the terms upon which the structure of liberalism and republicanism had been built in 1931. Many of them lived to see their dreams turn to dust, other grew cynical, some were killed, some died in exile. But their contribution to the cause of liberal Spain remained like seed in winter earth, awaiting better times and renewed hope, while their contribution to the thought and art of all mankind was indisputably significant.

Writers in Revolt

One of the greatest thinkers of modern times and in many ways
the moral conscience of the Generation of '98 was Miguel de
Unamuno y Jugo (1864–1936). Although he was a Basque, born
in Bilbao during a time of renewed Basque nationalism, Unamuno considered himself a Spaniard first, even going so far as
to advocate the use of Castilian in place of his native Basque
tongue. But this was only the first of the paradoxes of which
Unamuno was to become the advocate. He was educated at the
University of Madrid, where he received a doctorate of philosophy. But his stormy opinions kept him from finding a teaching
position in his chosen field. At last, in 1891, he was given a chair
in Greek at the University of Salamanca. Nine years later he
was appointed rector of that university, a position he held
until the end of his life.

Unamuno's position, expressed in newspaper articles and
short, acidly witty books, was one of constant intellectual revolt against authority of any kind. He was an enemy of the
Spanish monarchy and a critic of the political parties of the
Republic as well. His opposition to and brilliant criticism of
the regime of dictator Primo de Rivera caused him to be exiled
to France in 1923. But when he returned, he did not cease to
attack the authority of the state, although the state was now

Miguel de Unamuno.

a republic. It seemed, indeed, that Unamuno's real political enemy was politics itself.

In his novels Unamuno parodied classical forms. To him, the vital and final sense of human existence is provided by the constant conflict between an individual's will and his spiritual passions. In his lyric poetry, this theme is again stressed. The poems seem to seek out opposition, strive to open a dialogue between poet and reader; for all life is a dialogue—the dialogue of conflict.

In 1913 Unamuno published a work of philosophy entitled *The Tragic Sense of Life,* in which he came to grips with essential problems of the Spanish conscience. In this most important work, Unamuno maintained that for the real man, for the complete individual, neither faith nor skepticism provided an adequate philosophical basis for existence. Man's unquenchable urge to live makes death and the hope of life after death his basic problem, whether he realizes it or not. Man's will demands that there be life after death, but man's reason discounts the possibility. A man must live with this tension and even learn to use it, to build systems of thought upon it. This is the essence of the tragic tension of life. Any solutions that seek to avoid this tension, to obscure it, or wish it out of existence can lead only to sterility. But our scientific age seems devoted to distracting man from the realization of his tragic condition, or to obscuring that condition beneath heaps of material "goods." Therefore, Unamuno remained pessimistic regarding man's immediate future; it would be sterile and boring at best. To counteract the drug of materialism, Unamuno urged that man develop a determined will to action—any action—in order to surmount his growing dependence on technique as an end in itself.

The master of paradox, Unamuno stuck to his position as rector of the University of Salamanca even as the waves of Civil War washed over the area. He stubbornly attempted to maintain a position of neutrality between the forces of the traditionalists and those of the Republic. But in the end, outraged by the inhumanity and anti-intellectualism of the traditionalists, the aged philosopher was moved to speak out against them—to their faces. While his international reputation kept him from assassination, he was made a virtual prisoner in his own house and died brokenhearted in 1936 as his beloved country tore itself to pieces.

The man who gave the name "Generation of '98" to his contemporaries and who influenced them as much as any other thinker was José Martínez Ruiz (1873–1967), who adopted the pseudonym "Azorín." Born in Alicante, Azorín became a journalist and was elected to the Cortés several times as a Republican candidate. Attracted by the theory of anarchism, he sought to apply it to literature and to literary criticism in his book *Literary Anarchists* (1895). By 1900 Azorín had adopted a more creative attitude and a more optimistic one. In *The Hidalgos* (1900) he tried to develop in essays the theme of the continuity of the Castilian spirit, especially as exemplified by the life of the Castilian peasant. Turning to fiction in 1902, he made a fictional character named Azorín the hero of several novels, and later adopted the name for himself.

Azorín's constant theme after 1900 was that the Castilian land has a soul. And Castile is the essence of all Spain, its timelessness evoked by the toiling peasantry. Becoming more conservative as he grew older, Azorín was elected to the Spanish Academy in 1924. His later books strive to achieve mythical universality. He described his efforts as an attempt to "put a new soul, a soul of our times, into old characters." Thereby he hoped to enrich the present with the past. As opposed to Unamuno and other radicals of his era, Azorín was attracted to the values of traditionalist Spain, though certainly not to its modern anti-intellectualism. Taking no part in the Civil War, he lived out a long life and died eventually in Madrid, at the age of ninety-four, in the midst of a new era of change.

Pio Baroja y Nessi (1872–1956) attempted several careers at once, but was successful only as a novelist. Born in San Sebastián (a Basque) he studied medicine and practiced for two years. Later he operated a bakery in Madrid. At the same time he ran twice as a Republican candidate for the Cortés and was twice defeated. His novels *The Basque Land* (1909), *The Fight for Life* (1904), and *Red Dawn* (1906) described his native Basque country, the struggles of the poor, and the sordid slums of Madrid. Later he turned to cosmopolitan historical fiction, but never achieved the power of his earlier work. His best novels are autobiographical, and in them the relation of thought to action is central. His ideas were revolutionary, his style clear and impersonal. Like Azorín he outlived his fame and died with his essentially pessimistic outlook evidently justified.

Less politically inclined, but of considerably greater stature as a writer was Juan Ramón Jiménez (1881–1958). Born in Andalusia, he studied at a Jesuit school and then at the University of Seville. Later he moved to Madrid to become a journalist and, in 1901, a staff member of the Free Institute. In 1916 he made a journey to the United States, where he met and married an American girl. With the advent of the· Civil War, Jiménez fled to Puerto Rico, where he taught at the University of San Juan and continued writing poetry.

Jiménez's earlier works are on the theme of spiritual love, and in style they avoid concrete expression for mystical evocation. Later Jiménez was to become more lyrical in a period of expression of his inner feelings. In 1914 he published a book of semi-fictional travels through Andalusia entitled *Platero and I* (Platero was the name of a donkey) which won him international fame. Awarded the Nobel Prize for poetry in 1956, Jiménez's last work returned to the mystical-spiritual themes of his youth.

Perhaps the best known, internationally, of Spain's modern philosophers was José Ortega y Gasset (1883–1955). Born in Madrid, he was educated at the Universities of Málaga and Madrid. He received a doctorate in philosophy in 1904 from the latter. He went on to study philosophy in Germany and in 1910 was appointed professor of metaphysics at Madrid University. Like Unamuno and Azorín, in his early years he made his views known to the world through journalism. His book *The Old and New Politics*, published in 1914, defined the attitude of the young Spain that was striving toward the Republic, and it was tremendously influential in rousing Spanish intellectuals against the monarchy. In 1915 he became director of the magazine *España* and in 1923 founded the magazine *Western Review,* both of which periodicals gave him a fine sounding-board for his political opinions.

When Primo de Rivera seized power in 1923, Ortega y Gasset renounced his professorship at Madrid University and actively entered politics. In 1931 he founded a small, independent Republican political group and was elected its representative to the constitutional assembly. But in 1933 Ortega y Gasset retired from political life, and when the Spanish Civil War broke out in 1936, he went to France and, ultimately, to Argentina.

In an early book, *Meditations of Quixote* (1914) Ortega y Gasset had defined man as "I am myself and my surroundings." Carrying his individualistic philosophy a few steps further, he published in 1930 one of the most influential works of the twentieth century, *The Revolt of the Masses.* The masses Ortega y Gasset had in mind were not the laboring classes. He divided men into two categories: the independent, cultivated man, and the mass-minded man. The mass-minded man demands nothing of himself and everything of the state (any state). He lacks self-evaluation and is content with mediocrity in all things. Furthermore, and this is a grave danger, he seeks to extend mediocrity everywhere. The twentieth century is witnessing the triumph of mass-minded men who have revolted against their previous masters. Ortega y Gasset offers as a solution the creation of a new intellectual elite minority who must lead and rule. A self-imposed exile from Franco Spain, it was not altogether surprising that Ortega y Gasset should consent to return eventually to his native land, despite its government. He died in Madrid.

Of all the Spanish writers of this century, none was more talented or better loved than the young poet Federico García Lorca. He was born in Andalusia in 1899 (and cannot therefore be counted as one of the Generation of '98) of wealthy parents. He studied law at the University of Granada and, later, literature at Madrid University. His first poems, published in 1921, show the influence of Jiménez in the musical quality of the verse. But García Lorca's inspiration was the folk legend and folk music of Andalusia. In his poems life is seen as dramatic destiny; man is dominated by passion and death; reality and unreality blend together as in a dream.

In his long poem "The First Gypsy Romance" (1928) all the images are real and concrete. But the tragic story is directed by forces of nature. In "A Poet in New York" (1929) García Lorca evoked the brittle despair of the city from the experience of a brief visit. In 1930 he turned his genius to the theater and created plays that have become modern classics, such as *Blood Wedding* (1933), *Yerma* (1935), and *The House of Bernardo Alba* (1936). García Lorca's particular genius was to combine universal themes with local reality, employ a style at once very learned and popular, and to rely upon the traditional as well as the new whenever the occasion seemed appropriate. A bitter critic of the ideas of traditionalist Spain, García Lorca was caught in the city of Granada in 1936 when Francoist forces rose to seize control. He was kidnaped one night, hurried away, executed, and his body thrown into an unmarked grave in a crime that cut short a brilliant career and shocked the civilized world.

Spanish Painters of the Twentieth Century

The flowering of genius in poetry, novels, and philosophy which marked the turn of the present century was matched by a rebirth of Spanish painting. It is hardly too much to say that Spanish painters have both created and defined the styles of art that have dominated our era.

Most famous of all contemporary Spanish painters, Pablo Ruiz y Picasso, was born in 1881 at Málaga. He studied at the Academy of Barcelona, and by the age of fourteen he had already mastered the styles of such Golden Age artists as Velásquez. His entire life since that time may be seen as a search for new modes of expression for an abundant talent.

In 1900 Picasso moved to Paris, and he has remained an expatriate ever since. In Paris he grew interested in primitive art, then becoming quite popular, as well as in archaic art forms of the ancient Mediterranean and pre-Columbian America. These influences, combined with respect for and interest in the techniques of the French master Cézanne, led Picasso to investigate the problems posed by three-dimensional design.

In an exhibit in 1908 Picasso hung paintings which were described as "cubist" by several critics because of their geometric design. But Picasso himself disapproved of the term. He had, he claimed, done no more than look at an object from several points of view at once.

After 1920 Picasso entered a period in which his figures

"Guernica," by Pablo Picasso.

were monumental and sculpturesque. His painting "Guernica" for the Spanish Pavilion at the New York World's Fair in 1937 summed up the agony and terror of the Civil War and indicted the forces of traditionalist Spain for a terrible crime against humanity. But despite his outspoken Republican views, he was not molested by the Nazis during World War II and continued to live and work in Paris.

To Picasso art and nature are two different realities—interrelated, but independent. Art is not a mere representation of nature. "Through art," he has said, "we express our conception of what nature is not." Though he has lived a cosmopolitan life and is universally important as a painter, Picasso is very Spanish in his use of violent color and abstract design and in his depiction of the continuing tension between sentiment and reality.

On extended loan to the Museum of Modern Art, New York, from the artist, P. Picasso.

Another founder of the Cubist school of modern painting was José Victoriano Gonzales (1887–1927), better known by his pseudonym Juan Gris. Born in Madrid, he studied engineering there. In 1906 he moved to Paris, where he quickly became friends with Picasso. His painting at this time has been described by Gris himself as "a sort of flat, colored architecture." He was influenced by Cézanne and Braque as well as Picasso, but later developed a more realistic style he called "Synthetic Cubism" which was all his own. His painting was becoming more and more lyrical, combining sensuousness with intellect, when death cut short his promising career.

Joan Miró, who was born in 1893 near Barcelona, was another member of the Paris expatriates. Going to Paris in 1920, Miró joined the Dadaist movement, which sought to ridicule outmoded forms and conceptions right out of existence. Exhibited in a group show with several surrealists in 1925, Miró's work won immediate recognition.

After the fall of Paris in 1940, Miró returned to Spain but moved to the United States in 1947. His work has since displayed increasing gaiety, color, and rhythm. In 1958 he was awarded the Guggenheim International Art Award.

The Spanish painter who has created the most controversy in recent times is, without doubt, Salvador Dali. Born in 1904 near Barcelona, Dali studied at the Madrid Academy from 1921 to 1926. His early work (until 1928) showed a heavy influence of Picasso and Miró. But his true sources are the Italian medieval metaphysical painters such as Chirico and Carlo Carra, who relied on the evocative powers of symbols. In 1929 Dali went to Paris and announced himself officially as a surrealist. When asked to explain his inspiration and method, he has described his paintings as "handmade photographs" and his method "the spontaneous method of irrational knowledge" based on "association of delirious phenomena." Actually, his paintings are brilliantly colored and composed, very precise

OPPOSITE, ABOVE: *Salvador Dali.* OPPOSITE, BELOW: *Joan Miró, with some of his paintings.*

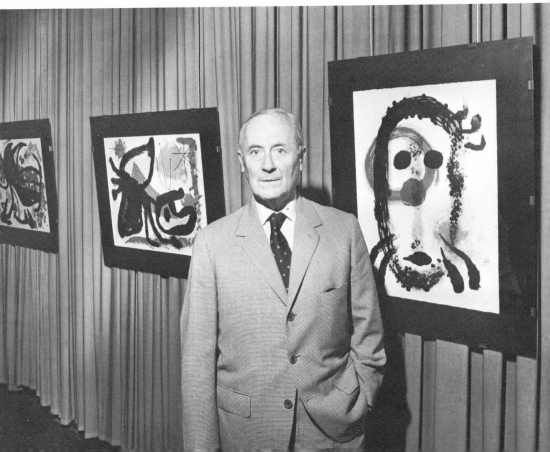

representations of different objects chosen for their supposed subconscious symbolism. They are photographs of dreams, calculated invasions of the viewer's forgotten memories.

No discussion of contemporary Spanish art would be complete without mention of the great musician Pablo Casals. Although Spain is exceptionally rich in varied folk music, Spanish composition over the centuries has not reached the heights of Spanish literature or painting. Aside from Manuel de Falla (1876–1946), who adapted folk themes to French impressionist modes, Spain has boasted no composers of the first rank. But Pablo Casals has, in our own day, become the world's greatest cellist.

Born near Barcelona in 1876, Casals learned to play the piano, the violin, and the flute by the age of four. Some time later he also learned to play the organ (his father was an accomplished organist and music teacher). By the age of five Casals had written his first composition. In 1888 he went to the Barcelona Municipal School of Music, where he studied the cello. In 1894 he was invited to perform before the royal court in Madrid and international recognition followed soon after. On trips to foreign countries (his first was in 1901) Casals has also conducted most of the world's great orchestras.

A man of deep social conscience, Casals organized a workers' concert association in Barcelona in 1920. During the Civil War he gave benefit concerts for hospitals and children in the Republican zone. With the downfall of the Republic he fled to Prades in southern France. He now divides his time between there and Puerto Rico and journeys throughout the civilized world on concert tours.

In 1945, when Premier Georges Bidault of France made Casals a Grand Officer of the Legion of Honor, he said, "You are one of the voices of the world's conscience." And in truth, the fate of Pablo Casals sums up the fate of those great Spanish artists of this century who still survive. They are voices of conscience, in permanent exile from their native land.

chapter ten

THE STRAITJACKET

In the harsh heat of the summer of 1939, Spain lay prostrate. There were at least 500,000 dead, close to 500,000 more had become exiles, and Nationalist prisons were estimated to hold nearly 200,000 political prisoners. Although the land itself had not suffered in the same way as the French countryside during World War I, nevertheless the cities had been badly bombed, villages were destroyed, communications wrecked, and thousands of farm animals slaughtered. That segment of Spanish industry that had escaped outright destruction was now worn out and obsolete.

More than that, the fury of the struggle had exhausted political passions among the Republicans, devitalized formerly militant workers, and reduced peasants to their former state of numb acquiescence. On the Nationalist side, complete political control was exercised by General Francisco Franco, now hailed as *Generalissimo* or *Caudillo* (leader), who was chief

Houses wrecked by rebel (Nationalist) planes at Toledo.

of state. The traditionalist coalition that had supported Franco
had been united in one basic aim, though bitterly divided on
many issues: to stop the clock of progress in Spain, to "freeze"
Spanish society at a level that would ensure its continued ex-
ploitability. And the Nationalist victory succeeded in achieving
that goal. For twenty-five years time stood still in Spain—or as
still as the ruling authorities could make it.

The Authoritarian State

For administrative purposes Spain is divided into fifteen regions
(corresponding roughly to ancient kingdoms and provinces),
which are in turn subdivided into fifty administrative provinces. The governors of these fifty provinces are appointed by
the government at Madrid and are directly responsible to the
national Ministry of the Interior. Local municipal councils in
small towns are elected by "heads of families," who alone have

the right to vote. But in towns or cities with a population of more than 10,000 the mayor is appointed by Madrid. Usually in theory, and almost always in practice, no decisions of any importance whatsoever can be made at the local level without approval from Madrid.

The Cortés was re-established by the Nationalists under a new constituent law in 1942. But it was a far different body from the Republican Cortés. It had 586 members, many of whom were appointed directly by the Nationalist government, others of whom were elected on the basis of a restricted suffrage. Elected members serve for three years; appointed members may serve for life. One-third of all members of the Cortés are elected by the syndicates—government operated, dominated and exploited institutions that replaced trade unions. In fact the Cortés is able to suggest laws only with the approval of General Franco. Its powers are almost nil.

General Franco, who is chief of state, is also prime minister, commander-in-chief of the armed forces, and head of the Falange party. A Council of State set up in 1941 to advise and assist the *Caudillo* was as helpless as the Cortes to act without his approval. There is also a Supreme Court, which in theory reviews government decisions in the light of basic laws but which in practice has inevitably acceded to governmental wishes. It will be seen then that political power in Spain certainly does not reside within the formal framework of government. It resides with the *Caudillo*.

The Falange party emerged from the Civil War with expectations that were never to materialize. The original radical fascist program of the party, which would have threatened the interests of monarchists, the rich, and the Catholic Church, was suppressed during the war and after it by the cautious Franco, who realized he could continue to rule only with the support of all these groups. Nevertheless, immediately after the war, and for so long as prospects of an Italian-German victory were good during World War II, the Falange was allowed to expand its membership tremendously. This also had the advantage (from the *Caudillo's* viewpoint) of submerging the fanatical minority of Falangists with a vast mass of opportunists. Every village had its Falange headquarters and every city block its Falange "boss" who spied on his neighbors and was responsible for their loyalty to the regime. The Falange had been turned into a convenient administrative-police machine completely at the disposition of whatever ideals Franco found necessary to propagate at any given time.

Under the Labor Charter promulgated by the Nationalists as early as 1938, Spanish workers were required to belong to various government syndicates. These syndicates included employers as well as employed and were part of the government, with representation in the Cortés. Of course they were absolutely controlled by the state, and most of their top personnel were required to belong to the Falange. Since the state existed to serve the interests of the very rich and the large industrialists, the Spanish syndicates almost always decided all questions in favor of employers. Strikes were absolutely forbidden. Workers who showed any sign of resistance to the syndicate's decisions could be simply fired, or they could be imprisoned. Those who showed too much rebelliousness were often executed.

The Catholic Church, which had, both nationally and by and large internationally, supported the Nationalist cause during the Civil War, had hoped to regain with Franco's victory the power and prestige it had lost during the years of the Republic. In this it was to be somewhat disappointed. A general system of public education was retained, although the Church was once again granted the right to run its own separate educational system. Besides that, a certain amount of religious instruction, conducted by priests or nuns, was injected into the public school system. The Church was granted a veto power over textbooks and teaching materials to be certain they contained nothing repugnant to Catholic doctrine. This influence, both direct and indirect, was extended to *all* education, including the university level. On the other hand, under the terms of the concordat (agreement) signed by Franco's government and the Pope in 1953 the right to nominate bishops was reserved to the Spanish state. It was also agreed that priests would receive a stipend from the government, thereby making them at least somewhat dependent on the whims of the state. Other religions were to be unrecognized by the government, and, although their rites might be celebrated privately, no public celebration was to be permitted. Divorce was simply declared illegal.

The Spanish Army (which, because of the accidental deaths of its top generals in airplane crashes and high casualties among officers during the Civil War, found itself completely under Franco's command) was rewarded for its victory over the Republic with a return of those privileges, appropriations, and dignities that had been withdrawn under the Republic. Despite the existence of a civilian government hierarchy to rule the various provinces, the captain generals of the larger regions of Spain

A high-school class in Madrid.

had the final and usually decisive say on many problems. Insults, real or imaginary, on the part of civilians toward the Army, or disobedience to Army regulations that affected civil life, were punishable before regular Army courts-martial. Even purely criminal cases, such as robbery, could be tried by military courts-martial if it was established that the accused had at any time been a member of the Army. Universal military service was established and two years' service in one of the armed forces made compulsory for all Spanish youth.

Needless to say, Catalan and Basque independence movements were ruthlessly stamped out. Leaders were executed, political activists imprisoned, and a cultural war undertaken against the heritages of both peoples. The Basque and Catalan languages were no longer to be studied in school, nor was any printed matter whatsoever, from newspapers to road signs, to appear in either Basque or Catalan. Furthermore, as special centers of Republican resistance during the Civil War, both the Basque provinces and Catalonia were subject to special punitive taxes and to direct military control of civilian activities.

Perhaps the most sinister aspect of the straitjacket forced onto Spanish society at the end of the Civil War was the execution of all those who were suspected of resistance to the regime. While official Nationalist figures yield a total of 84,000 persons executed from 1939 to 1942, there is good reason to believe the number was closer to 200,000. From the former president of Catalonia, Luis Companys, to the humblest worker who was suspected of leftist opinions, the pattern was usually the same. The condemned spent his last night on earth squatting on the stone floor of the prison chapel. At dawn he was gagged (so that his cries would not arouse the populace), thrown into a truck, and driven to a nearby cemetery. There he was machine-gunned on the lip of his own grave.

Over the years Spain's political straitjacket was to be fitfully loosened and tightened in response to internal economic neces-

Two members of the Guardia Civil *(national police) in Madrid.*

sity and the fluctuations of international events over which
Spain had no control. By and large, during the years of World
War II, Spanish domestic repression or the easing of it reflected
the varying fortunes of Germany and Italy and their prospects
of success against the Allies. After the war it was often a reflection of the necessity to make Spain acceptable to those European nations on whom she depended economically and of
the cold-war politics of the United States.

The Impact of International Pressure

When the Civil War came to its bloody end in the spring of
1939, Nationalist Spain was the nominal ally of Germany and
Italy—the two powers whose assistance had been vital to
Franco's victory. Furthermore, the continued existence of the
Nationalist regime, with its fascist overtones, seemed to depend
on the continuing success of fascism on the international scene.
When Germany and Italy went to war against England and
France, Franco's government declared itself neutral—on the
side of the Axis powers. Spanish airfields were made available
to German planes and Spanish ports to German U-boats. After
the conquest of France, Spanish raw materials helped to feed
the German war machine. The fact that Spanish forces took
no active part on Germany's behalf at the time was not due
to caution or unwillingness, but to the fact that Spanish industry was exhausted and Spanish military supplies were piti-
fully inadequate for modern warfare.

On September 23, 1940, General Franco and Hitler met at
the town of Hendaye on the French border. To the German
dictator's demands that Spain actively enter the war against
England (France had already been conquered) Franco did not
disagree. Instead he raised conditions. First of all the Spanish
Army and Air Force would have to be re-equipped; secondly,
various Spanish ambitions in North Africa, such as the taking
over of French Morocco, would have to be satisfied. Hitler
found these demands exorbitant at the time (later he was to

Generalissimo Francisco Franco.

tell Mussolini that he would rather have "several teeth extracted" than go through another interview with the *Caudillo*). But a tentative agreement was reached to permit German units to pass through Spain in order to conquer British-held Gibraltar. However, during the next few weeks Italian forces suffered heavy defeats in Greece and North Africa and the Italian fleet was savagely mauled by the British at Taranto. Ever cautious, Franco postponed the operation against Gibraltar, and kept postponing it thereafter.

When Nazi Germany invaded Russia, Spain signed the anti-Comintern pact with Italy and Germany. Later a Spanish "volunteer" division—the so-called Blue Division—was dispatched to share the disasters of the German army in Russia. But when the German war machine ground to a halt in Russia and when, with the entry of the United States into the war, Axis hopes seemed doomed, Franco's policy accommodated itself to realities. In secret negotiations with the British, Franco swore on November 8, 1942, to remain neutral, thus enabling the Anglo-American armies to land in North Africa.

With the Allied victory over Germany and Italy in 1945, Spanish internal as well as external affairs passed into a state of crisis. Most of the people of the victorious democratic nations had assumed that, with the downfall of Hitler and Mussolini, Franco too would be overthrown, if not from within, then through direct military pressure from without. These expectations were shared too by the remnants of the Spanish Republican government, which had spent the war years in exile (primarily in Mexico), and also by various groups of dissidents within Spain. Spanish monarchists, feeling that the moment was auspicious for the return of Don Juan, son of Alfonso XIII, called upon Franco to resign. Various Republican leaders approached the British, French, and American governments with plans for an uprising in Spain to be supported by the Allies. The French government ominously closed the Spanish border. Tension gripped Spain.

But nothing happened. The war-weary Allies could not be persuaded to embark on yet another liberation. The monarchists could count on almost no popular support within the country, nor were the oppressed masses in any condition to make an uprising. In frantic attempts to make the Spanish regime somewhat less odious in foreign opinion, and to tranquilize opposition at home, Franco promulgated in 1945 a new *Fuero* of the Spanish People, which was a proclamation of individual liberties and rights. Of course the publication of this liberal document did little to alter actual conditions in Spain. Personal liberties and rights continued to be disregarded. The new *Fuero* was intended primarily for foreign consumption. It did not, however, prevent the United Nations (on February 9, 1946) from formally and severely censuring the Spanish government. At the same time all member nations broke off diplomatic relations with Spain. Nor did the passing of a new Act of Succession in 1946, by which Spain was declared to be a monarchy, with Franco acting as chief of state and regent (with no king named nor any date set for an end to the regency), serve to rehabilitate the Nationalist government in the eyes of the world. It was not so much the superficial reforms undertaken by the Spanish government that won it eventual recognition and acceptance in the international community as it was the strategic and political needs of the United States in the cold war against Soviet Russia.

In the new era of nuclear warfare and intercontinental bombers, the United States required airfields in Spain as part of the security program it had designed to protect itself and western Europe against possible Russian aggression. A role in cooperating against Russia suited Franco domestically, since it seemed to validate his continual claims to have saved Spain from communism and to have been an early and unsung anti-communist crusader. With American military leaders much more concerned with American security than with the nature of Spanish internal government, concessions might be wrung from Washington. In this calculation, General Franco was correct. Negotiations (which had proceeded secretly for some time) were publicly opened in the autumn of 1951. After one and a half years of stubborn bargaining, the United States won permission to set up three air bases and a naval base in Spain, while Franco got promises of financial and diplomatic aid.

While heavy bombers of the United States Strategic Air Command now circled over Spanish skies, the American government supported Spain's bid to be admitted into the United Nations. With the failure of the policy of ostracism, foreign ambassadors had long since begun to return to Madrid; and by 1955, when Spain was taken into the General Assembly of the United Nations, her international acceptance was complete. But the intervention of America into Spanish affairs was to have much more profound results than simply diplomatic acceptance. Probably unsuspected by Franco, it marked a decisive turning point in Spanish affairs. It resulted in changes to the Spanish economy and a loosening of the authoritarian straitjacket that could not be revoked. With the arrival of the Americans on the Spanish scene the clock of progress started ticking again. Much as they might hate it, Spanish traditionalists could do little to prevent ensuing events, and, unfortunately, the Spanish people could do little to control them. A new look came over the face of Spain.

chapter eleven

THE NEW LOOK IN SPAIN

There are some Spanish economists who maintain that the intervention of the United States was not decisive in bringing the Spanish economy, by 1963, to what they refer to as the "take off" point—that level of production from which further expansion is self-generating. They point to the fact that the more than one and one-half billion dollars poured into the civilian economy between 1953 and 1963 and the even larger sum granted for the modernization of Spanish armed forces represent only a small part of the twelve-billion-dollar-per-year Spanish gross national product. Yet it would seem that American aid provided the extra stimulus needed. In any event, the growth of the gross national product, which in the late fifties was a healthy 4.5 percent per year (about equal to that of the United States), reached a startlingly successful 7 percent per year during the 1960s.

It was this economic growth that undermined the authoritarian state constructed by traditionalist Spain. By enlarging the middle class and raising the expectations of a better life among workers and peasants, economic progress forced a basic alteration in the rigid political framework in Spain. Political, social, and even cultural progress now became inevitable.

The Expanding Economy

The problem faced by Spanish industry in the years following the Civil War was basically one of markets. With a domestic standard of living too low to provide an outlet for many manu-factured goods, and with foreign markets more or less closed during the period of international ostracism, Spanish industry stagnated at pre-Civil War levels of production. Added to this handicap was the graft-ridden inefficiency that resulted from the bureaucratic central control exercised over industry by the Falange and other governmental organs. Imports were heavily taxed, and government control of foreign sales and currencies resulted in Spanish manufacturers receiving about half the amount of money their goods brought in from those few foreign markets open to them, with the government pocketing the other half.

Beginning in 1951, however, with the reopening of all foreign markets and the direct assistance of the newly vitalized N.I.I. (National Institute of Industry), Spanish industry began a remarkably rapid climb to higher production levels. The N.I.I., with the authority of the state behind it, commenced a planned program to expand those basic industries, such as steel, electric power, and mining, upon which any expansion in the consumer industries would have to be based. Furthermore, also according to plan, such basic factors as communications and transport were to be modernized. The N.I.I.'s accomplishments in these fields have been dramatic. Hydroelectric projects, such as that on the Ebro River, increased electric power output ten times over; cement production (essential for construction industries) rose 39 percent between 1953 and 1956 alone; during the same

A truck factory in Madrid.

period pig iron production increased 14 percent. Much of Spain's antiquated railroad rolling stock was replaced, and up to 50 percent of her 11,243 miles of track modernized. A similiar percentage of Spain's 82,000 miles of roads were re-paved. The output of commercial vehicles (especially trucks vital to industrial transport) climbed from near zero in 1951 to 54,000 per year in 1964. And (while it is not a basic industry, it does reflect the jump in industrial capability) the production of passenger automobiles rose from 12,000 per year in 1953 to more than 120,000 per year in 1964.

With the revitalization of Spain's basic industry and the consequent rise in production, light and consumer industries were also established or modernized. By 1964 radios were being produced at the rate of 575,000 per year, television sets at the rate of 443,000 per year, washing machines at the rate of 300,000 per year. While these totals seem miniscule by American standards, they are impressive for industries starting at near-zero levels of production in a nation of low incomes and living standards.

Agricultural production, in spite of the establishment of chemical fertilizer plants and a big increase in the output of farm tractors and machinery, remained below levels reached before the Civil War in 1936. This was due in part to the natural difficulties of managing Spain's depleted soil, but also to the archaic land-ownership structure. The great landowners of Andalusia, who had backed Franco, remained in control of huge and relatively unproductive areas; the small independent farmers of Castile and other regions suffered from high taxes and low government-controlled prices for their produce. Furthermore, the monopolization of food distribution by several large companies that took fat middlemen's profits increased the price of food in the cities and resulted in lower consumption. From 1953 to 1963 a large percentage of American aid had to be devoted to the importation of foodstuffs and was consequently not available for industrialization, its primary purpose.

Nor was the N.I.I.'s program of industrial expansion put through without setbacks and without pain. The flood of American dollars and N.I.I.-sponsored foreign investments in Spain that occurred after 1953 brought on a ruinous inflation. In 1956 the peseta was officially pegged at twenty-eight pesetas to the dollar but was actually valued at over sixty pesetas to the dollar on the black market. Black marketeering in money was not restricted to individuals, but was carried out also by the largest corporations and banks in Spain. The period of industrial expansion from 1953 to 1963 was a black marketeer's paradise. Besides foreign loans and investments, Spanish industry required heavy domestic financing. Since individual savings accounts in Spain were all but nonexistent, financing came only from the largest banks and industrial trusts. This led to a concentration of ownership in Spanish industry that amounted to monopoly. And as this concentration was in the hands of the rich, who both directly and indirectly controlled the government, they were able to raise or lower prices at will, thereby forcing out smaller companies and raising the cost of living.

The import of modern machinery from abroad and the immediate gap caused by low exports during the first throes of industrialization forced Spain to seek loans from European countries as well as the United States. But these nations would not lend the Spanish government money until they were assured of responsible management of Spanish finances. This led, in 1959, to relaxation of controls on the value of the peseta so that it became freely convertible into other currencies at the rate of sixty pesetas to the dollar. It led also to modest and totally ineffectual attempts by the government to control or break up the large industrial trusts and limit the investments of Spain's leading banks.

Other sources of imbalance in the Spanish economic structure were the sudden increase in the import of such foreign goods as whisky, cars, gasoline, and cigarettes on the part of the rich, and the tendency of the rich to transfer their wealth to other more secure currencies and places. The obvious solutions of raising import taxes and establishing a realistic graduated income tax and truly effective monetary controls were politically impossible to a regime backed (and partly composed of) the industrialists, landowners, and bankers who would have to be restricted.

In spite of Spain's economic boom, the problems faced by the Spanish economy remain the same. Either a much larger domestic market will have to be created by raising wages and living standards within Spain, or additional foreign markets will have to be opened. With a new taste for the amenities of modern life, Spanish workers are now pressing for better living conditions. The Spanish government, at the same time, is faced with the necessity of entering the European Common Market, the only possible outlet for Spain's increased industrial output. Both of these drives have led to political upheavals and political changes of far-reaching consequences during the past decade.

The Political Scene

The essential facts of the current Spanish political scene are fragmentation of the traditionalist coalition that brought Franco to power; revival of political interest and ambitions among workers and peasants; the necessity for liberalizing the government to make it more acceptable to the democracies of the European Common Market with whom it will, in future, have to be associated; and the cautious, tardy, and hesitant steps being taken by the Spanish government to cope with these facts.

The first victim of industrialization in Spain was the Falange. With an active membership overwhelmingly composed of opportunists, petty racketeers, and bureaucrats who did little work while fattening on the public payroll, the Falange became an obstacle to the development of industry and hence an enemy to the rich industrialists. Falangist control of syndicates, public corporations, and government offices that had to deal with industry became an insufferable source of inefficiency, corruption, and nuisance to large manufacturers and the conservative rich, as well as a block to foreign trade. Under pressure from these groups, the government began easing Falangists out of important jobs as early as 1953, suppressing demonstrations by Falangist students at the universities and undermining the political power of the party. While occasional lip service was paid to Falangist ideals, by 1967 the party had lost all its power and was no longer a serious factor in Spanish affairs.

Of perhaps greater permanent importance was the gradual transformation of the government's syndicates into real labor unions. In spite of the fact that they were staffed at the top by government directors and dominated by employers, the lower levels of syndicate organizations, in the factories and white-color offices, began to fall into the hands of workers who were determined to use them to improve their lot. Since the rich now had a heavy stake in industrial peace and efficient production, the government could no longer wage open warfare against strikes. Beginning in 1957 and with gathering momentum, strikes for higher wages and better working conditions were called by workers in defiance of government regulations and the instructions of their own syndicate leaders. The shipyard workers of Bilbao, the machine-tool workers of Barcelona, transport workers, miners, and many others began to go on strike. While there were individual cases of violence on the part of government police, the authorities in most cases preferred to negotiate with the strikers. In industry after industry Spanish workers won at least part of their demands. These victories led to growing confidence, and a renewed realization of their latent power, on the part of Spain's working classes. Several political groups, some new, some old, tried to channel or seize control of this growing political power.

The Spanish Catholic Church, under the impact of liberal directives from Rome, and because of its realization that it had lost all contact with the vast majority of Spaniards, had been struggling for some time to escape its captivity to the Franco regime. Since the Catholic Church had supported traditionalist Spain during the Civil War, there was a touch of irony in its attempts to disassociate itself from its past. Ironical or not, Catholic leaders knew that their course of action during these years might be their last chance to retain the allegiance, even nominally, of the awakening Spanish people. Catholic priests began a campaign during the late fifties to win the support of their bishops for an active role in labor unions—and were surprisingly successful. *Opus Dei* (Work of God), a political-

Violence erupts during a workers' strike in Barcelona.

Carlists cheering Dutch royalty after the marriage of Prince Don Juan Carlos to Dutch Princess Irene.

economic action group led by Catholics, both lay and ecclesiastical, campaigned for greater economic liberalism, for higher wages and greater benefits for workers, and, in the case of the Basque and Catalan clergy, for more local independence. Priests were now to be found aiding workers during strikes and even marching with them during demonstrations in Barcelona and other cities. Definitely not revolutionary in outlook, *Opus Dei* hoped to preserve traditional aspects of Spanish society by persuading the government to grant the working classes social justice before they were moved to seize it for themselves.

Closely allied to *Opus Dei*, there arose in the late fifties the Christian Democratic movement headed by Gil Robles, former leader of Spanish conservatives during the Civil War. Proposing the re-establishment of a constitutional monarchy (with either Don Juan as king or his son Don Juan Carlos) *after* the termination of the Franco government (presumably upon General Franco's death), the Christian Democrats sought also to preserve traditionalist values by liberalizing the government before it collapsed or was overthrown. Technically illegal (since all political parties except the Falange were banned), the Christian Democrats, counting on support from industrialists, bankers, and large landowners, were able to influence the government toward more efficient administration, elimination of corruption in its fiscal and economic policies, and at least a token liberalization of political repressions. By 1960, after a series of amnesties and pardons, it was estimated that not more than two thousand political prisoners remained in Spanish jails—a figure shocking enough by democratic standards, but a sign of greatly increased tolerance in traditionalist Spain.

Somewhat to the left of the Christian Democrats is the Democratic Action group headed by Dionisio Ridrueja, a reformed Falangist and poet. Counting among its supporters various liberal intellectuals and reformist-minded businessmen, as well as some labor leaders and a few survivors of the Republican past, Democratic Action sought a return to republicanism— but, again, only after the Franco regime came to a natural end. With a liberal social and economic program and an idealistic view of the possibilities of parliamentary government in Spain, Democratic Action bore certain uncomfortable resemblances to the liberal middle-class parties of the thirties, which were unable to rally the more militant masses to their support.

Both Christian Democrats and Democratic Actionists are tolerated by the regime as semiformal organizations, almost political clubs. Not at all tolerated and with a following that cannot yet be assessed are the reborn socialists and communists. There is no doubt that large underground networks of these parties exist. Furthermore, both parties maintain offices abroad and claim to inherit the mantle of leadership of the now vanished generation that fought the Civil War.

The Social Scene

The undermining of traditionalist Spain has progressed much further socially than politically. Again this is in large part due to an influx of foreign ideas and foreign tourists, as well as a rising standard of living and the loosening of the governmental straitjacket.

The mass-information media such as radio, television, and the press remain under state control. But in recent years press censorship has been relaxed. Spanish newspapers are now permitted to print news of the outside world as it actually happens. They are also permitted to print criticism of the Spanish government on a local level and even criticism of the national regime, provided it is couched in general and not specific terms. No criticism whatsoever is permitted of General Franco or other high state officials, of the Army or of the Church. But neither are the papers now required to fill their pages with endless praises of the *Caudillo*. The press has come a long way since that day in 1945 when one Spanish newspaper, *Arriba*, headlined the Allied victory over Germany: "Victory for Franco!"

The cultural war against the Basque provinces and Catalonia has also been relaxed. Novels and poetry may now be printed in Basque and Catalan, and various symbolic gestures toward recognition of their cultural heritage have been made by the Madrid government. Neither language is yet taught in the public schools.

Social mobility is on the rise in class-bound Spain. While the rich remain as remote as ever from the rest of the population, the middle class and the workers—their mutual suspicions somewhat purged by years of Civil War and dictatorship and a common interest in reform—now increasingly mingle in a way that would have been considered impossible barely twenty years ago. Recognizing the fact that only through support by Spain's working class can their own progressive goals be achieved, educated young middle-class Spaniards are increasingly involving themselves in labor movements and demonstrations.

The old, strict Spanish code of morality, both public and private, is also undergoing change. While officials of the Catholic Church inveigh against sleeveless dresses, daring bathing suits, mixed swimming, and contraception, Spanish fashions follow those of the rest of the world, beaches on the *Costa Brava* and *Costa del Sol* look much the same as beaches on the Riviera or Florida, and Spaniards increasingly practice family-planning. While divorce is still all but unobtainable, marriages celebrated by other religions are now recognized. Furthermore, in 1966, the government announced that henceforth Spain's thirty thousand Protestants and five thousand Jews would be able to celebrate their faiths publicly as well as privately.

The sale of foreign magazines and books has increased tremendously. While the censorship occasionally bans foreign news magazines when they contain articles considered too damaging to the Spanish government, a free circulation of foreign ideas predominates. American movies are very popular, especially westerns and musical comedies. While any meaningful control over their political destinies has not yet been granted to the Spanish people, a certain illusion of freedom, of partnership with other countries, of participation in modern popular culture is maintained by the relatively free influx of ideas, students, and, above all, tourists from the outside world.

An excellent parable of Spain's changing social structure and private morality was Luis Buñuel's film *Viridiana*. Buñuel, Spain's greatest film director, had been in voluntary exile since the Civil War. But he was invited back after the liberalization of the fifties to make a film on Spanish soil. The film he made is a searing account of a young nun who, in attempting to bring Christian kindness and social justice to a group of crippled beggars, is the victim of the inherited rage, frustration, and corruption of what Spanish history has made these men. In the end, her task hopeless, her convictions shattered, her faith gone, she abandons the idealism of traditional virtues for the reality of sensual pleasure. But the audience is left to decide whether she will be any happier thereafter.

Costa Brava, *on the Mediterranean coast in northeast Spain.*

chapter twelve

SEEDS OF THE FUTURE

More than in any other European nation, Spain's future belongs to her youth. The generation that would have been moving into positions of leadership today was effectively destroyed, dispersed, or demoralized by the Civil War and the years of harsh repression that immediately followed it. Between Spain's ruling generation in government, industry, and politics, and the university generation of today there is a tremendous gap. This gap is not to be measured solely in years; it is also to be measured in terms of hope, anger, commitment, and energy. Today's young generation of students and workers owes no debt of allegiance to either disintegrating traditionalist Spain or the Republican movements of the thirties. It has not been scarred by war, nor has its energy been sapped by the bitter decades of the struggle for mere survival. The problems Spain has inherited from her stormy past will be theirs to solve. Before we examine these problems and their potential solution, let's turn to the generation that will have to solve them.

The Midcentury Generation

Spanish university students (and their young instructors) are today in the forefront of Spanish political life. Student demonstrations involving thousands and ending generally in outright clashes with the police are now a common feature of life in Madrid, Barcelona, and other big cities. What are the immediate complaints that have led Spanish students to risk imprisonment, beating, and, occasionally, death?

To begin with, the students find conditions intolerable within the universities themselves. And they quickly recognize that the immediate burdens under which they must pursue their education are only reflections of basic faults in the Spanish regime. Overcrowding in university residences—with students jammed into outgrown and outdated quarters—reminds them of the slum conditions under which so many Spaniards live in the larger cities. The lack of books and equipment (libraries are understocked, laboratories old-fashioned and poorly equipped, playing fields almost nonexistent) reminds them of the obsolescence of much of Spanish industry, of the essential backwardness of government commitment to economic progress. The poor pay received by their instructors is but a reflection of the improverishment of the lower middle classes generally.

Nor is material poverty within the university the only or even the most important source of dissatisfaction. Spanish students, who come into contact with foreigners as often as or perhaps more often than their parents, are aware of educational standards in the outside world. They are vividly aware of what the search for truth means. But censorship, Church domination of teaching materials, and the outright falsehoods with which the government has, from time to time, tried to feed their inquiring minds have made it all but impossible for them to receive an education that would be recognized as even adequate in other nations. The ingrained fear that the government displays toward free intellectual inquiry and the clumsy obstacles it places in the path of all who pursue truths that might be harmful to the status quo is but a shadow of the essential repression still symbolized by the Madrid regime that extends to all areas of Spanish life.

As early as December 1955 and January 1956, demonstrations had taken place in the University of Madrid. In response, the government had certain students dismissed from the university and others arrested and brought to trial. An ominous fact emerged from the student trials: many of the student leaders were actually sons of Falangists, Nationalists, and conservatives who had helped to erect the traditionalist state. Traditionalist Spain was losing its heirs.

The suffocation of the student demonstrations of 1955 and 1956 had the effect of awakening the students to the fact that, unless they found allies, they would be powerless to win reforms. Therefore, in June 1959, when various underground elements called upon Spanish workers to stage a general strike throughout the country, Spanish students went from door to door in working class districts in Madrid, Barcelona, and elsewhere urging the workers to participate in the strike. The

OPPOSITE: *Madrid University students demonstrating on campus in May 1962.* RIGHT: *University students flee from police during campus disturbances in January 1967.* BELOW: *The students take cover behind the statue "Passing the Torch," by an American sculptress, and hurl rocks at charging police.*

strike never came off, for various reasons. But Spanish students had had their first taste of real political action and had formed their first links with the workers. Many were imprisoned for their activities; many became afraid of the consequences of them. Classes graduated and new students appeared. But the generation of protest was a continuing process.

In February 1962 student demonstrations again broke out at Madrid and Barcelona. They have rarely ceased since, and now their political nature has matured and become apparent. Portraits of General Franco are burned, and shouts for the overthrow of the government are heard. Nor do the students march alone. Now their ranks are joined by workers and increasingly by priests. Their dedication and determination cannot be doubted. But now, in these immediate years, their abilities will be tested by problems that their fathers were unable to solve and that haunt Spain today.

The Economic Problem

In 1962 Spain formally applied for admission into the European Common Market. While her application must, according to the rules of the member nations, wait its turn behind that of England, it seems certain to be considered within the near future. Entry into the Common Market seems the only way to ensure the new Spanish industry of sufficient markets to support its growth rate. But at the same time, entry would open Spain to a flood of duty-free imports from other countries. Can Spanish industry compete? Only by keeping its workers on subsistence wages or by drastically increasing efficiency. However, a raise in wages to European levels would be demanded of Spain before she was admitted. The rich and the big industrialists are therefore of two minds regarding the Common Market. If Spain joins the Common Market and they have not yet taken steps to increase efficiency, they must inevitably be swamped by competition from Germany, France, and Britain.

Another reason, and the determining one, for entry into the

Common Market is to ensure the continuance of a market for Spain's export agriculture, primarily citrus fruits. Although Spain remains the primary producer of citrus fruits in the Mediterranean, other nations such as Greece, Israel, and Algeria are now offering keen competition. Since the Common Market is their only potential customer, they must accept prices and quotas imposed by the Common Market's buyers. The big landowners of Andalusía welcome any reinsurance of their market they can gain by joining the Common Market. But will they welcome also the imposition of new and more up-to-date standards of pay and working-living conditions for their peasants that Common Market economists will demand?

Unless the economic forces of traditionalist Spain are willing to accommodate themselves to the modern world. Spain's entry into the Common Market could convert the country into simply a source of raw materials and a dumping ground for the manufactured goods of other member nations. Spain would become, in effect, an economic colony of Europe.

One possible way to strengthen the Spanish position would have been to attempt to organize a Spanish-American Common Market with the nations of South and Central America. These underdeveloped countries, presently dependent on the American economy, would have welcomed an alliance with Spain as an entry to the European market. Spain might, in that case, have acted as a sort of economic broker between South America and Europe. But since most South American governments remain content to exist as caretakers of American economic interests, to achieve this goal Spain would have had to support revolutionary movements throughout South America. And the traditionalist government in Madrid was in no way interested in supporting revolution anywhere.

Spain's entry into the Common Market will come about within the next ten years. Spanish youth, allied with progressive forces throughout the country, has therefore little time to try to reach solutions that will keep its country from sinking into colonial status.

The Political Problem

The Law of Succession to the Spanish Throne, which was originally promulgated by General Franco in 1945, has been modified several times since then. Essentially its provisions remain the same. Spain is a kingdom. Franco is chief of state, acting as regent in the absence of the king. The king, who remains uncrowned, of course, is either to be Don Juan, son of Alfonso XIII, or Don Juan Carlos, grandson of Alfonso XIII. Don Juan is personally odious to Franco and has but rarely been permitted to enter Spain (and then in semisecrecy) during the past decades. Don Juan Carlos, on the other hand, has, by agreement with his father, received his education in Spain. If the monarchy is to be restored then, it would seem that Don Juan Carlos will be king. But the likelihood of the monarchy being restored grows fainter with each passing day.

The opposition parties of the older generation—Christian Democrats or Democratic Actionists—could probably be persuaded to swallow a return to monarchy. But these parties do not represent either the aspirations of the working class and the peasantry or the hopes of Spanish youth. They have no confidence in the supposed constitutionalism with which a future monarch might reign. They see the monarchy as a rather tattered front for the forces of traditionalist Spain—forces that cannot solve Spain's economic or international problems.

The most biting international problem of the moment in Spain is its role as a partner of the United States in the continuing American effort to contain communist expansion in Europe. Most Spaniards realize that if ever war should break out between the United States and Russia, no matter what Spanish authorities might say about it, American strategic bombers would take off from Spanish bases with nuclear war loads. And the Russians would undoubtedly strike those bases. Since the bases are within a few miles of Madrid, Saragossa, Cádiz, and other important cities, much of metropolitan Spain would be wiped out. There is little doubt that almost any Spanish government, except a traditionalist one, would immediately cancel its agreements with the United States as regards the bases. This was the single most important factor in continuing American support for the Francoist regime. The association of the United States with Franco has earned it the growing enmity of those forces that will one day inherit or seize power in Spain.

The deepest political problem in Spain today is the fact that there is no single political organization (or coalition) which really represents the scattered forces of opposition: disgruntled lower middle class, workers, students, peasants, and intellectuals. When and if such an organization arises, it will be able to take power. The question is, Will it be able to take power peacefully or will a new civil war break out? This depends almost entirely upon the Spanish Army.

Although the Spanish Army, which numbers 350,000 men, has been re-equipped by the United States (it even boasts six wings of F86F Saberjet fighter planes), it remains antiquated. While it would be of little use in an international conflict, the Army is powerful enough to win a civil war within Spain itself. However, with the introduction of universal military service in 1940, the Spanish Army became no longer the hard group of professionals it once was. It is now by and large a citizen army, its ranks composed of young workers, students, and peasants. Whatever decision the traditionalist officers' corps may make, it is extremely unlikely that most of their men will ever open fire on their own families, their own people. History has demonstrated that draftee or citizen armies do not make good suppressors of revolutions. Nor could the armed forces of traditionalist Spain necessarily count on American support. The changes in American world strategy and weaponry of the last few years have reduced the value of America's Spanish bases to a point at which they are probably not worth fighting over.

Aside from the lack of any solid and cohesive organization to represent antitraditionalist Spain, the factor that more than anything else prevents rebellion is the searing memory of the horrible cost of the last civil war. This is a theme on which traditionalist Spain never tires of harping. And it is effective with those who remember. But the new generation in Spain does *not* remember the agony of the thirties. And they have examples of national liberation revolutions throughout the world since World War II to encourage them.

Many observers consider Spain to be in a prerevolutionary condition. But it is likely that, if and when revolution occurs, it will be remarkably peaceful. It is extremely unlikely that there will be a renewal of civil war in Spain if only because Spanish traditionalists no longer have the means or any real desire (except among a small handful of diehards) to wage it. Compromise may restore the Spanish monarchy, but if so, it will be purely decorative. If traditionalist Spain shows the slightest sign of using the monarchy to maintain repression, it will go.

When they come to power, today's younger generation in Spain must still grapple with immediate and difficult problems. Everything in this ancient nation must be rebuilt. Land must be given to the peasants. Workers must be given a much higher standard of living. New democratic forms must be erected within which personal and collective liberties are guaranteed. Solutions must be found to the continuing desire of Basques and Catalans for home rule. Modern social and educational codes and standards must be adopted, but, hopefully, without undermining that which is most precious of the Spanish past.

The problems are enormous, and time is rapidly running out. Will solutions be found? The heritage of Spain's heroic past and the fine temper of the Spanish people indicate that they will.

FOR FURTHER READING

Alvarez del Vayo, Julio. *Freedom's Battle*. New York: 1940.
———. *The Last Optimist*. New York: 1950.
Borkenau, Franz. *The Spanish Cockpit*. London: 1937.
Brenan, Gerald. *The Face of Spain*. London: 1950.
———. *The Spanish Labyrinth*. New York: 1943.
Buckley, Harold. *Life and Death of the Spanish Republic*. London: 1940.
Casado, Segismundo. *The Last Days of Madrid*. London: 1939.
Cot, Pierre. *The Triumph of Treason*. New York: 1944.
Feis, Herbert. *The Spanish Story*. New York: 1948.
Gironella, José. *The Cypresses Believe in God*. New York: 1955.
Goldston, Robert. *The Civil War in Spain*. New York: 1966.
Hemingway, Ernest. *For Whom the Bell Tolls*. New York: 1940.
———. *The Fifth Column and Other Plays*. New York: 1939.
Koestler, Arthur. *Spanish Testament*. London: 1937.
Malraux, André. *Man's Hope*. New York: 1938.
Matthews, Herbert. *The Yoke and the Arrows*. New York: 1957.

Menendez Pidal, Ramón. *The Spaniards in Their History.* New York: 1950.

Mora, Constancia de la. *In Place of Splendor.* New York: 1941.

Orwell, George. *Homage to Catalonia.* London: 1938.

Paul, Elliot. *The Life and Death of a Spanish Town.* New York: 1939.

Regler, Gustav. *The Owl of Minerva.* London: 1959.

Sender, Ramón. *Seven Red Sundays.* New York: 1936.

Souchere, Elena de la. *An Explanation of Spain.* New York: 1964.

Taylor, Francis. *The United States & the Spanish Civil War.* New York: 1956.

Thomas, Hugh. *The Spanish Civil War.* New York: 1963.

INDEX

DATE DUE			
			ALESCO